LUTHER AND THE REFORMATION
An Illustrated Review

M · L

IN SILENCIO ET SPE ERIT FORTITVDO VESTRA

Luther:
a 1529
portrait by
Lucas Cranach
the Elder

Luther
and the
Reformation

AN ILLUSTRATED REVIEW

by HANNS LILJE
in collaboration with Karl F. Reinking

AMERICAN EDITION
Translated and edited by MARTIN O. DIETRICH

FORTRESS PRESS   **PHILADELPHIA**

AMERICAN EDITION

First published by Furche Verlag H. Rennebach KG (Hamburg, 1964)
under the title MARTIN LUTHER:EINE BILDMONOGRAPHIE

TABLE OF CONTENTS

That Man Luther

The sixteenth century, the watershed of modern history, involves more than the Reformation, and the Reformation involves more than Luther. Why then does the figure of this man tower so prominently in the foreground?

One reason is that Luther was the initiator of the great work. This distinguishes him above the significant men with whom the sixteenth century was blessed. It is true that although Zwingli won his insights without Luther, he later on was quite open to his influences, without fully accepting Luther's positions. Others, like Bucer, Blaurer, Bugenhagen, cannot even be imagined without Luther. This applies even to Melanchthon, by far the most excellent mind of the Reformation and Luther's cherished friend, and to Calvin, whose lofty systematizing and organizational ability advanced the work of the Reformation into areas which Luther would never have reached. Not one of these men regarded himself as anything but a student of Luther.

But more is involved in Luther's prominence than chronological priority. A profoundly factual reason elevates Luther above these men. This reason becomes apparent when one compares the personalities from still another angle. Calm and profound Humanist thinkers like Erasmus and Thomas More stand in the forefront, but despite the profundity of their thought and intention, they were really nothing but intellectual aristocrats. The fame of Erasmus throughout Europe was only that of a scholar. He was followed by men of action, like Calvin and Ignatius of Loyola (who must be mentioned in order to intensify the comparison). These were the great organizers who molded the labor of their lives into historically effective forms.

It is immediately evident that Luther was neither just a thinker nor just an organizer. His life was the very battleground on which the fundamental issues of the Reformation were fought through to their conclusion. The very things which he suffered through, prayed through, struggled through, and attained in faith, were the realization of the goals toward which the Humanists and Calvin, the great organizer, aspired and labored. In short, Luther's struggle for his faith had vicarious significance. He himself had neither a philosophical program nor world-spanning organizational plans. He was simply himself, went his own way, and fought to its conclusion the demands of faith. It is for this reason that he is so personal, that his labors cannot be appreciated if detached from his personal life, and why he stands before us with greater vitality and immediacy than the systematizers and organizers. It just does not make any sense to speak at this point in terms of weakness or greatness, about limitations or significance. Personal directness was his contribution to the Reformation. In this he was God's instrument in the course of history.

It is imperative, therefore, to focus our attention on his development, not in order to expose some psychological secrets, but to discern the significance of that life in which those historic decisions were made which determined and shaped not only the Reformation but an entire era of western history.

His life stands out in bold relief when contrasted with the lives of many of the political personages of his day, with men such as Francis of France or Henry of England! They and others like them spent a lifetime seeking only their own welfare on the grand scale which their station allowed them. They did not seek the welfare of their people, and they did not disguise their own selfishness. And there were many others—churchmen and scholars —who were drawn along in the same stream of ambition and egomania. Luther stands out in contrast to them because he was a man who had suffered. The view of Luther as the heroic warrior is completely wrong if heroism is interpreted in the shallow sense of the latter part of the nineteenth century; Luther was not a "hero" in this bourgeois sense. His exemplary and vicarious significance lies in the fact that in his search for God he wrestled with death and the devil. That his personal wrestling extended beyond him and took on a universal significance encompassing all the powers of the historical world and ultimately altering the foundations of Europe, was not deliberately planned by him. These things happened because he was an instrument in the hands of God. Luther himself expressed the secret of how God shapes the course of history when he said that God had led him into all these things "like a blind horse." This expression is one of reverence at the inscrutability of the divine will. In a number of forceful and striking remarks Luther showed that he was fully aware of the basic difference between the Renaissance conception of a great man and the divine calling in life which made him an instrument of God's will. He himself said, "My first request is that no one should mention my name, and call himself Lutheran, but Christian. What is Luther? After all, it is not my doctrine. I have not been crucified for anyone. In I Cor. 3, 4, 5, St. Paul would not permit Christians to call themselves Pauline or Petrine, but Christians. What have I, a poor, stinking bag of maggots, done that the children of Christ should be called by my unholy name? My dear friends, let us be done with this, let us delete these sectarian names and bear the name of Christian, since it is his doctrine that we call our own." The accent therefore lies not on Luther but on the gospel, not on the historical, romantic remembrance of a person but on Christ's presence.

One of the most difficult but fascinating tasks entailed in presenting the life of Luther is the unfolding of the paradoxical circumstance that while, on the one hand, he is a true representative of his time, on the other hand, he is also a lone individual. If we are to understand Luther correctly, we shall have to give special consideration to both aspects of his appearance on the stage of history: the fascinating epoch of the early sixteenth century, and the person of Luther as it develops an almost explosive activity.

The earliest published picture of Luther, the title page from the *Sermon Preached at the Leipzig Castle on the Day of SS. Peter and Paul in the Eighteenth Year*. In the original the inscription is also in reversed mirror-writing.

The Ninety-five Theses

On October 31, 1517, the day before All
Saints, in the city of Wittenberg on the
Elbe River, in the Electorate of Saxony, the
following occurred: A monk named
Martin Luther, member of the Order of
the Augustinian Eremites, appointed
Doctor of Theology, Professor at the
University of Wittenberg, District Vicar
over the monasteries of his chapter in the
Electorate of Saxony, and preacher at
the City Church, wrote two letters. One
was to the Archbishop of Mainz, the
Elector Prince Albrecht; the other was to
the Bishop of Brandenburg. In these
two letters (the one to Archbishop Albrecht
is still extant) Luther protested against
the charlatan and false conception of the
indulgence as it was proclaimed in word
and practice by the Dominican monk
John Tetzel in behalf of an indulgence
for the construction of the new St. Peter's
Church at Rome. Luther wrote further
that all this was taking place on the basis
of instructions issued and printed in the
name of the Archbishop. He requested
the Archbishop to undertake changes.
To both letters he attached ninety-five
theses in which, in a scholarly manner,
he explained how dubious the notions
being disseminated by Tetzel about the
essence of indulgences were, and in accord
with the "old custom of scholars" he
extended an invitation to discuss them in
an academic disputation. Considering
the circumstances of those days, the news
of what these theses by the Wittenberg
monk had to say spread throughout
Germany with incredible rapidity. The
theses unleashed a movement destined
to assume world-wide and historical
dimensions: the REFORMATION.

A page of the book edition of the *Ninety-five Theses*.

The Castle Church at Wittenberg

The day on which Luther made these Theses public was of particular significance for the Electorate of Saxony. All Saints Day was the date of the widely-known indulgence festival in Wittenberg. Luther's reigning sovereign, Elector Frederick of Saxony, was a pious man who was indefatigable in his endeavors to make of the Castle Church a treasure-house of holy relics. The Elector had obtained indulgences from the pope for the benefit of his Church of All Saints at Wittenberg. These indulgences brought in considerable revenues which were used largely to finance the Elector's recently founded university. A year before, on October 31, 1516, Luther had preached rather circumspectly concerning the indulgence. His Theses of 1517 now touched upon areas of interest which extended beyond religion into the world of power politics and large-scale financial operations. In this way he came into conflict with a highly explosive combination of issues which were also of concern to the common man in his anxiety for the salvation of his soul.

The Castle Church
at Wittenberg,
detail from a
woodcut by
Lucas Cranach
the Elder.

11

The Impact of the Ninety-five Theses

1517: On October 31, the Theses were made public in Latin. Luther's letters to Archbishop Albrecht of Mainz and to the Bishop of Magdeburg, directed against Tetzel's indulgence preaching, remained unanswered.— Luther sent letters to a number of scholars and friends inviting them to a disputation.— The Theses were reprinted in several cities. Hand-written copies as well as reprints were quickly disseminated. (Two copies of the Theses in poster format from Leipzig and Nürnberg as well as one in booklet form from Basel are still extant.) The Theses were translated into German.—Amazed at their effectiveness, Luther, in the winter of 1517-1518, began at once to draw up a popular treatise in German dealing with the basic ideas of the Theses, the *Sermon on Indulgence and Grace*.—The mood with which Luther's appearance on the public scene was welcomed in many quarters was reflected most strikingly in the exclamation of the Franciscan prior John Fleck: "He who will do it has come!"—That which Luther did not directly intend to bring about by his action against the

The indulgence trade, detail from a drawing by Hans Holbein the Younger, used in a pamphlet.

indulgence sermons of Tetzel, had now happened: The reformation of the medieval church, which had long been in the wind, had now begun! It could no longer be turned back.

1518: The conflict became more intense.—Tetzel accused Luther of heresy and received the support of his order.—The convention of the Saxon Chapter of the Dominican Order resolved to charge Luther before the pope with suspicion of heresy.—In the meantime Archbishop Albrecht had forwarded the Theses to Rome.—Luther's own order indirectly made the Theses the subject of discussion at its convention in Heidelberg in 1518.—At the end of April, Luther, incognito and on foot, traveled to Heidelberg with a letter of recommendation from his Elector designed to protect him against open threats of persecution.—Honored and looked upon as an intellectual marvel, his personal prestige and stature were definitely enhanced in the course of the Heidelberg Disputation.—Age and youth were divided in their opinions and attitudes toward Luther's views.—Upon the advice of Staupitz, the vicar of his order, Luther sent his *Explanations of the Ninety-five Theses*, the *Resolutiones*, to Pope Leo X.—The Dominican Order, charged with responsibility for the inquisition and the suppression of heresy, managed to initiate disciplinary proceedings against Luther in Rome.—The Theses were condemned as heretical.—On August 7 Luther was summoned to appear in Rome within sixty days.—A sermon delivered by Luther on May 16 concerning the nature of the papal ban induced Cardinal Cajetan, papal legate to the Diet of Augsburg, to intervene in the dispute centering on Luther.—Emperor Maximilian wrote to the pope.— Cajetan called upon Elector Frederick the Wise to surrender Luther, whose person and cause were now enmeshed in a major political power play.—Elector Frederick and the pope were in agreement about rejecting the plan of Emperor Maximilian to designate his grandson, Charles I of Spain, as his successor. Upon the request of Frederick the Wise, the citation for Luther's appearance in Rome was modified into a hearing by Cajetan at Augsburg.—Faced with death at the stake, Luther departed for Augsburg.— The interrogation by Cajetan from October 10 to 12 remained fruitless. —Luther finally appealed "from the pope poorly informed to the pope who is to be better informed," and rejected his judges as prejudiced and uninformed.—Staupitz released him from his vow of obedience to the Augustinian Order and then left Augsburg.—By his hasty flight from the city Luther avoided the threat of arrest.—On October 31 he was back in Wittenberg.—On October 25 a renewed request for Luther's extradition arrived from Cajetan in Augsburg.—Luther offered to emigrate voluntarily from Electoral Saxony.—In anticipation of the papal bull of excommunication Luther, on November 25, appealed to a general council of the church.— Luther invited his friends to a farewell dinner.—At the last moment a letter from the court preacher Spalatin prevented his departure.—On December 18 the decision was finally made. Frederick the Wise wrote to the pope that he would not surrender Luther nor banish him from Electoral Saxony unless he were convicted of heresy by scholars and impartial judges. An important reprieve had been won for Luther.

1519: Political intrigue now came to the forefront.—In January the pope again attempted to win the political collaboration of Elector Frederick the Wise to prevent the election of Charles I of Spain as the successor to Emperor Maximilian.—In the name of the pope, a Saxon nobleman, Karl von Miltitz, conferred the Order of the Golden Rose of Virtue upon the Elector. At the same time Miltitz attempted to initiate a reconciliation between Luther and the Curia.—Emperor Maximilian died on January 12.— The great tug-of-war over the succession now began between the Elector, the pope, Francis I of France, Henry VIII of England, Charles I of Spain, and the financial might of the Fugger banking house. On June 28 the struggle came to an end with the election of Charles V as the German emperor. The decision—also in the Luther affair—now lay in the hands of the newly elected emperor, who remained in Spain until the autumn of 1520.—At the same time that the emperor was being elected at Frankfurt, the disputation long awaited in the academic world between Professor Andreas Karlstadt, a Wittenberg comrade-in-arms of Luther, and Professor John Eck of Ingolstadt, a former friend of Luther, now took place not only in the presence of, but with the participation of, Luther.—Because of his expertise in the technique of debate Eck succeeded in getting Luther to expose himself more fully than ever before, not only in the matter of the indulgences and the ban, but also concerning the recognition of the ultimate authority of the councils and the primacy of the pope.—In the course of this year Luther's position became progressively clearer through numerous publications of a pastoral nature—Luther developed from being a theological debater on the issue of indulgences into the reformer of the entire edifice of the Christian faith.

Left:
Woodcut from the title page of Hutten's polemic against the burning of Luther's writings in Mainz.

Right:
A book illustration showing Luther as he burns the papal bull.

1520: This was to be the year of major decisions.—On January 9, under the chairmanship of the pope, the College of Cardinals decided to resume its proceedings against Luther.—Partisanship in behalf of Luther's cause now began to extend beyond the circle of theologians and scholars.—Franz von Sickingen, the spokesman of the German knights, offered Luther his castle as an asylum in the event that he should need such protection against Rome. A similar offer was made several months later by groups of noblemen in Franconia.—It became evident that many groups no longer viewed Luther's battle as a purely religious affair but as an issue with national implications and related to the matter of reforms desired in the empire.—On June 15 the papal bull *Exsurge Domine* with its threat of excommunication appeared. It set a limit of sixty days within which Luther was to submit.—As an introductory countermeasure Luther composed his letter *To the Christian Nobility of the German Nation,* which was published in August.—Two papal emissaries, Jerome Aleander and John Eck, attempted to persuade the emperor and the German princes to carry out the provisions of the papal bull.—Prodded by Aleander, Emperor Charles V in September forbad the heresy of Luther in his Burgundian ancestral lands.—In October Luther's writings were burned in Louvain and Liege; in November, in the cities of Cologne and Mainz.—On October 10 the papal bull reached Luther. —Luther's second major polemical treatise appeared: *The Babylonian Captivity of the Church.*—On October 23 the coronation of Charles V took place at Aix-la-Chapelle.—In November Luther published the Latin treatise *Against the Accursed Bull of the Anti-Christ,* and the German booklet *The Freedom of a Christian.*—On November 17 Luther called upon the emperor and the empire, the princes and cities, to join him in his appeal.—Efforts were now under way in the political arena to place the Luther affair on the agenda of the forthcoming imperial diet.—On December 10, two months after the receipt of the papal bull and after the expiration of the time limit set for Luther to recant, a notice written by Melanchthon was posted at the Parish Church of Wittenberg inviting students to attend the burning of books of canon law and scholastic theology. Luther personally cast the bull threatening him with excommunication into the fire.—The emperor went to Worms, where the imperial diet was to meet.—On December 29 Luther, in a letter to the Electoral court preacher George Spalatin, declared that without regard to life or death he would comply with the imperial summons to come to Worms.—The question of the Reformation's fate had now been raised.

1521: A feverish excitement gradually took hold of the general public and helped to influence the impending discussions of the diet.—On January 3, in Rome, Luther is finally excommunicated through the bull *Decet Romanus Pontifex*. The church had thus taken her ultimate step.—On January 28 the emperor opened the diet. Behind the scenes of the discussions concerning the administration of the empire, the reform of the imperial supreme court, and other urgent matters of state, the tug-of-war between the several factions took place over whether or not Luther was to be

Book illustration of Luther's appearance at the Diet of Worms.

16

summoned to Worms. The Curia did all in its power to block this.—On February 22 the emperor finally yielded to the estates of the realm. The citation was drawn up on March 6 and delivered on March 11 to the imperial herald Casper Sturm.—In the midst of final conciliation efforts by Glapion, the emperor's father confessor, heated polemical writings, advice pro and con by friends and neutrals concerning whether to go to Worms, Luther began his journey to that city on April 2.—He arrived in Worms at ten o'clock on the morning of April 16. On the seventeenth he was conducted before the emperor and the diet.—Two difficult days followed, for, as Luther was forced to ascertain, the issue was not that of an examination of his writings but solely the question of his recanting. He requested a day's delay. On April 18, at a plenary session of the diet, he defended the spiritual position of his religious insights. He refused to recant.—A very last attempt was undertaken by the estates of the realm to persuade Luther to accept a compromise. It was in vain.—April 26 was the day of his departure. Once again Casper Sturm was his imperial escort.—The emperor added the finale by imposing the imperial ban.—This shocked the German people less than the reports that Luther had been either captured or murdered. Luther's cause had now become the concern of all Germans.

Frankfurt on the Main
April 28, 1521

I bless you and commend you to God. I am letting them put me away and hide me, though I myself know not where. Though I would have preferred death at the hands of the tyrants, and especially as the victim of the raving Duke George, I still cannot reject the advice of good people, at least until God's own time comes.

I thought his Imperial Majesty should have brought together a Doctor, or perhaps fifty, and should in all honesty have reasoned with the monk and persuaded him. The only thing that was done here was to ask him: Are these your books? Yes. Do you want to retract them, or not? No. Then go away. O how blind we Germans are, how childishly we behave, and let the Romanists make such pathetic fools of us.

. . . It is necessary to be silent for a while and to suffer. A little while you shall not see me, and again in a little while you shall see me, as Christ said (John 16:16). I am hoping that it will be like this now. May God's will—the best of all—be done in this matter, as in heaven and earth. Amen.

Letter written by Martin Luther after his departure
from Worms to the painter Lucas Cranach at Wittenberg.

The Rebellion of the Imperial Knights

Luther had spent the year 1521 in "protective custody" in the solitude of the Wartburg, where he busied himself with the translation of the New Testament. Because the religious enthusiasts had caused disturbances in Wittenberg in the fall, he felt compelled in March of 1522 to leave the Wartburg and return to Wittenberg. In the western part of the empire the tragedy was being forged that was to result in the downfall of the two leading representatives of the German knights: Ulrich von Hutten and Franz von Sickingen. Even before the diet Hutten had urged an open revolt of the knights in favor of the Reformation and of political reforms. In the middle of the summer Sickingen, with a large contingent of soldiers, engaged in warfare with the Archbishop of Trier. The attack on Trier failed. Hutten fled to Switzerland while Sickingen retreated to his Castle at Landstuhl. The princes counterattacked and laid siege to Sickingen's castle. The latter was wounded and died on May 7, 1523, as the victorious princes stormed into the castle.

The Ebernburg Castle,
headquarters of
Franz von Sickingen,
woodcut by
Jost de Negker.

The Stage of History

The Political Scene

What was the world like that was confronted with Luther's message?

The most important concept from the early days of the Middle Ages, namely, the idea of emperor and empire, was now beginning to wane. Its splendor had disappeared when the Hohenstaufen line of emperors became extinct and had been replaced by the ontological natural law of High Scholasticism. The developing national states of Europe emerged with ever more distinct profiles, first in France and England, and then in the claims to sovereignty put forward by other states, city-states, and republics.

But the other prominent concept of the western world—the papacy—had also faded and lost much of its substance. The Babylonian Exile, which compelled the Vicar of Christ to move to Avignon, basically resulted in severe ideological harm to the prestige of the pope. For if it were possible to simply shift the geographical location of the seat of Peter's successor, then his universal spiritual position was also endangered. The schism had made internal church problems so visible that they could not be disguised. Europe's complex of states had now begun to assert its particular national sovereignty over against the universalism of the papacy.

Within the total scope of this development the German phase was only a peripheral phenomenon, and yet at the same time it constituted a very typical example of this emancipation process, in the course of which the central authority of the German kingdom and with it the universal validity of the German empire as well, began to crumble.

It is a curious quirk of history that three monarchs of greater than average stature appeared simultaneously and intimately interrelated on the European scene, all of whom personified this historic change in the power structure: Charles V of Hapsburg, the solemn, almost always self-controlled emperor; Francis I, the usually undisciplined, glamorous king of France, who might have become one of France's most distinguished rulers if he had not been so unrestrained; and finally Henry VIII of England, the most vital of them all, whose conceptions of kingship and politics, of the church and of marriage, exceeded all limits of credibility.

Finally, the great and threatening outsider, the Turkish Grand Sultan Soliman II injected himself so powerfully into the scene during his reign (1520-1566), that the entire political arena of those decades was dominated almost completely—apart from the series of popes—by the personalities of these same monarchs.

The Renaissance, with its interest in the total development of the individual personality with all its emotions and characteristic traits, had also awakened an interest in the human portrait. As a result, in almost all of Europe at the turn of the sixteenth century the art of painting in the specialized area of portraiture attained a pinnacle probably never again equalled. This is why we have portraits of the above-named monarchs which were painted by the leading painters of that day and which, with a high degree of characterization skills and extreme exactness, preserve the individuality of their personalities, their strengths and weaknesses. These very favorable circumstances enable us to visualize the outer appearance and inner qualities that radiated from these men.

All three had a somewhat astonishing characteristic in common: each of them had to overcome a considerable measure of inner insecurity when he came to power. But one should not forget that when these sovereigns began their reigns they were still relatively young men who were suddenly confronted with tasks which were to lead the internal as well as the external affairs of their countries toward crucial junctures of their history.

Francis I was undoubtedly a bold warrior and strategist. Some of his early surprise victories gained for him European renown and substantial success in his successive struggles against Charles. But in the actual affairs of state he was so uncertain that he gratefully accepted the quiet but firm leadership of Diana of Poitiers, who was his mistress though she was his senior by six years. This very feminine woman, whose likeness has been preserved in a portrait by Clouet, aided him with her understanding and counsel, thus helping him to arrive at his regal decisions. In those days no one considered it improper for her to come to the aid of her relatives and numerous friends with many generous favors.

Henry of England was unsure of himself to the highest degree. During his entire reign he occupied the stage of history with bluster and apparently tyrannical absolutism, but behind the scenes those conniving creatures were busy at work whom he himself had almost invariably elevated from less important posts, and who now effortlessly toyed with him as long as they knew how to observe correctly certain psychological rules of the game. The moment they committed a faux pas in this respect, there was no mercy for them and they fell with the same relentlessness that they had applied in toppling others before them. But there was always someone who held sway over Henry VIII. All his life he was nothing but a figurehead.

Charles was also insecure. This was a characteristic peculiar to the Hapsburgs, and among the later members of this dynasty—especially those from Spain—was destined to soar to the level of abnormality. But even more effectively than Philip II, his son and successor on the Spanish throne, Charles knew how to master this psychic flaw: Around his inner insecurity he constructed the very presentable protective shell of majestic dignity. His formal refinement, indigenous to the Burgundian court milieu so highly esteemed by him, and which later on was to develop into that overly refined artistic ceremonial in vogue at the Spanish court, was the way of life most suitable to him. This solemn dignity enabled him to avoid making rash decisions, for in this atmosphere no precipitous actions were possible. But then, since he repeatedly, though only after painful hesitation, was finally emboldened to make genuine decisions to which he was wont to adhere with remarkable tenacity (as in the case of people who find it difficult to come to a decision), he really presented the picture of a sovereign endowed with undeniable regal dignity.

But there was something else even more essential, since it concerned not his private life but the princely aspect of his person: He remained aware of the value that should be attached to the word of a sovereign. There is a world of difference between the English ruler whose temporary whim dictated when he would give and when he would break his word, and the young emperor who at Worms rejected the quite plausible and politically realistic admonition that he do away with Luther at once, regardless of the imperial letter of safe-conduct. He is supposed to have said that he did not want to blush with shame as did his predecessor Sigismond at Constance. It can also be said in his favor that in opposition to the wish of Duke Albert, the grave of Luther remained undisturbed at the express command of the emperor.

But he was also great—particularly when compared with the other two— in his stature as a statesman. While Francis always really stood at the head of France more like a cavalier and platoon-commander whose daredevil exploits often earned him good fortune and then, finally and embarrassingly, also misfortune, and while Henry VIII managed his kingdom like a large private enterprise that belonged to him and served him profitably as long as one was not too punctilious in the choice of methods (he was one of the wealthiest princes of his day), one discovers in Charles V a conscious awareness that the crown implies a vocation, in fact, an office which must be administered with a sense of responsibility toward history and God.

Specific and concrete tasks forced him to think on a large scale. It was a proud but truthful aphorism that the sun never set on his empire. Portugal and Spain were the two European powers for whom the new geographical dimensions of the universe, resulting from the discovery of the New World, signified a political reality. More will be said of this later. Even when limited to the area of the western world as it was then generally known, it is immediately obvious that the historic mission assumed by Charles is much more extensive than that borne by the other two. Henry ruled over a mere four million people, a rustic, self-satisfied community with a rather limited horizon and which in almost all essential aspects of life still had by no means divested itself of the Middle Ages. Aside from a small, flourishing strata of Humanists who stood in some relationship to Oxford and Cambridge and who were imbued with a genuine European consciousness, the rest of England was nothing but the northwestern frontier of the western world, enveloped climatically and intellectually in fog.

France with its population of fourteen million was already quite differently incorporated into the intellectual, cultural, and political history of Europe. Yet even when the French king constantly and actively intervened in the history of Europe by marching across his three borders—to the Netherlands in the north, Burgundy in the east, and above all to Italy in the southeast—what actually did his royal existence amount to when compared with the gigantic, far-ranging tasks that faced Charles? For several decades the conflict with France for the hegemony of Europe compelled Charles V to seek his battlefields in Flanders or Brabant in the north, or in Burgundy, or especially in Italy. But prior to these there were decisive wars with Spain itself, struggles to establish the inner unity of Greater Spain. Then came the bold, far-reaching battles with the Mohammedan pirate states in North Africa; some of Charles' most brilliant victories were won along the Algerian coast. Added to all this were the continuing martial conflicts with the ever more seriously threatening Turks in the eastern part of the empire. Would the menacing hammering of these eastern foes at the portals of the empire in the sixteenth century ever have provoked a person in England to listen and give heed? Yet here lay one of the serious political and military tasks, far graver than the Wars of Succession and the other piratical raids of the average European monarchs!

And then there was the controversy with the Reformation. For Charles this was a responsibility directly incumbent upon him as the bearer of the crown, with a twofold obligation for him who wanted equally to defend the authority of his political power as well as the endangered unity of Christendom with whose supreme secular office he was invested.

This one fact must now be made very clear, even though it is generally the most difficult for the modern observer to grasp: In Charles the concept came to life again that the emperor was entrusted with the supreme secular office in Christendom and that he was therefore obligated to solve the problem facing Christendom and to solve it in Christendom's behalf. The tragedy which surrounds the life and work of this ruler lies in the fact that in his mind's eye the idea of Europe's unity and the oneness of Christendom once again came alive and that despite his hesitating temperament and slowness in arriving at decisions, he took it upon himself to serve a historic mission in faith and to sacrifice the blood of his people, even though the idea itself had begun to be an anachronism.

It was a symbolic moment when in 1556 Charles V appeared before the princes assembled in Brussels to inform them of his decision to abdicate. As he entered he leaned upon the shoulder of the young Prince of Orange-Nassau, who soon thereafter was to lead the Netherlands out of the Hapsburg federation of states and into a totally new era of political and religious independence—a declining and an ascending epoch represented in two persons in such proximity!

In the mighty erosion process of the Middle Ages, the political powers were the first to deteriorate. The German empire, which represented the directive force and the concept of orderly power in Europe, went into a gradual decline. It had been a political system with a magnificent philosophical ideal, for to it belonged not only Germans but also Bohemians, Italians, Netherlanders, and Danes. A new balance of power now developed between the budding national states, the innumerable minor Renaissance principalities and city-republics of Italy, and, on the other hand, the church-state which equally strove to attain a secularized autonomy. It was this historic power play which was at the root of the conflicts, the alliances, the peace pacts, broken treaties, and new wars.

Parallel to this a profound structural change in the economic and sociological system of the old medieval form of society could be observed. Feudalism lost its meaning and its power to shape society. A new social order rose from among the free citizens of the cities, the patrician families, the members of the guilds, the officials of the burgeoning territorial and communal authorities and strove to acquire political leadership. New human ideals, which were no longer derived from the hierarchical structures of the society of the Middle Ages, became discernible. Italy took the lead. It was in the Italian city-states that the new principles were first understood and formulated. The most famous book of this type is Machiavelli's *The Prince*. One is always astonished to note how at such an early stage a clear and completely unemotional mind grasped the laws governing the modern power state and formulated them in a cool, sober-minded, crystal clear, and lucid form, completely independent of traditional Christian—or other—concepts.

One seeks in vain for the clarity and statesmanlike culture of the early Italian city-republics among the princes, the very persons who later on were to become the bearers of Europe's political development. Though their actions seem based less on careful reasoning and thus more awkward, they nevertheless occupy a remarkable place at the beginning of the sixteenth century. We are actually moving in the direction of the national state. It is quite normal that such a century-spanning development should impinge on the consciousness of the participants at very varying levels of clarity.

Italy with its city-states could not be the bearer of this development; it lacked the inclusive political unity. Among the few excellent minds who realized this was the very unpopelike Pope Julius II, who more than any other Italian of his day championed the cause of Italian unity.

But what Italy was unable to accomplish was present in very significant initial stages in France as well as in England. Without fully realizing it themselves, the two oftmentioned rulers laid the foundations for the future prominence of their two states and their continuing development into modern national states. Enough remained for their successors to accomplish: what Francis I started was continued by Henry IV, and was finally completed by Richelieu and Louis XIV. The early steps taken by Henry VIII were augmented by Elizabeth and Cromwell in a manner that made possible England's dominant position in the world thereafter. But the first steps had been taken.

It is obvious that the German territorial princes could not remain untouched by this development. Though they can be blamed for it, they demonstrated an amazing loyalty to the ideal of the empire. In order to evaluate this loyalty fairly, one should learn to view in reverse the well-known fact that the Holy Roman Empire of the German nation died of old age in 1806. It is astounding that despite its continuing weaknesses, the idea of the empire proved to be an authoritative bond for such an extended period of time, until, in fact, it simply could no longer be maintained.

Now it is possible for us to see in these early stages of the national state that the serious political crisis of the empire-concept, of the deterioration of the political unity of the western world, and of the emergence of a new political system took place independently of the Reformation. One simply cannot charge the Reformation with the breakup of European unity. This fact is of such importance because this development was by no means only "political" in the external, technical sense of the word, but also because it entailed a spiritual significance fraught with weighty consequences.

The empire-concept of the Middle Ages was based on the rigid parallelism of spiritual and secular power. The emperor and the pope were to each other as the sun to the moon. That there were involved disputes as to who represented the sun and who the moon is so well known that we need not go into detail here. But it was never forgotten that they belonged together. The idea that had its origin in the philosophy of history of the late nineteenth century, namely, that the emperor should never have paid attention to the pope and as a matter of principle should have disregarded the church, represents a most extraordinary and gauche application of modern judgments—and not very distinguished ones at that—to an entirely different historical era. ✓This juxtaposition of emperor and pope—regardless of the direction the balance of political power took—was simply the expression of the total inner unity of the western world and endowed the emperor as the sovereign ruler with a metaphysical sanctity. The office of the emperor was a divine office, and herein lay its prestige and authority.

When this juxtaposition, which was accepted as a normal situation, began to slacken toward the end of the Middle Ages, serious consequences were inevitable. Along with this process the metaphysical sancity of the emperor's position was bound to be jeopardized. The significance of this uncoupling can be recognized in a new set of problems that now arose and dominated the subsequent decades and centuries. It is the issue of the divine right of kings. This matter deserves very special attention. To an ever increasing degree the thesis advanced by Machiavelli now became the subject of thorough and theological deliberation. But it could now be perceived that the authority of the ruler no longer occupied its previously accepted rank in a metaphysical order of things, but had become a problem in itself. Two centuries later a totally secularized absolutism arose and became its logical heir.

This process of mutation and the rise of a new political order in the world can be observed most clearly in the case of another group that had once been very powerful: *the knights*. Their fate was truly tragic because this once outstanding class simply and silently ceased to exist. There was no longer any place for them in the new world that was unfolding. Such figures as George von Frundsberg, the prominent leader of the lansquenets, supplied a dignified finish to their era—but again only as military leaders and no longer as knights characterized by a specific ethic encompassing much more than mere martial weaponry. Figures like Franz von Sickingen and Ulrich von Hutten were already living anachronisms. Sickingen's noisy appeals simply made manifest before the world that wherever he raised his voice there was only emptiness. Hutten effectively symbolized the end of his own and of all knighthood by switching to the most modern vocation and becoming a journalist—with all the advantages and very obvious weaknesses of this vocation. Whatever survived of the ideal of knighthood was limited to the special privileges of a class; the genuine rights vanished.

The world of knighthood perished not because of a change of political ideology but because of a basic restructuring of the economy and of society.

The essential factor is to be found in the basic change brought about in the *economic order* by the new importance attained by money and the monetary system. It was an embarrassing fact for the landlords that since the end of the fifteenth century real estate was no longer the main element of their possessions; very noticeable competition was offered by assets in the form of negotiables, namely, by money. The worst effects of the monetary system, which even at this time precipitated a severe economic crisis, did not manifest themselves until the latter half of the sixteenth century, when Spanish gold and other precious metals from the New World began to have an effect. In the subsequent fundamental change in the European economic system (which did not occur without severe crises and upheavals), the knights lost their importance and were replaced by their more fortunate competitors, the cities.

But behind these political powers, those which were dying or outmoded as well as those coming to the fore, there emerged a new giant. At first this giant's rise was slow and his profile indistinct, yet gradually he became recognizable and was seen increasingly everywhere. This giant was the *national state*.

The external political form, to be sure, remained unclear for a long time. For a moment a national consciousness was discernible that appeared to be almost modern, but then it sank back and was submerged in the unchanged medieval concepts. It is true that at the Council of Constance in 1415 a division was already made on the basis of *nationes* in order to nullify the numerical preponderance of the Italians, but this was still far removed from the nineteenth-century concept of nationality. When the Hussite disputes erupted in Prague, the Germans living there naturally cast their votes on the side of the Czechs, just as the dissenting Bohemians sided with the Germans from the empire who inclined toward the Hussites. For a long time it was not regarded as unusual for the much sought armies of German mercenaries—especially the cavalry and the lansquenets—to fight each other. And the fact that Francis I and Henry VIII both deemed themselves eligible to wear the German crown and openly voiced their candidacy for it, might have been viewed as being provocative and ridiculous because of their personalities, but not because of their foreign nationality. But in contrast to these customs of long standing, the consciousness of a national individuality occasionally broke forth in quite unexpected and yet forceful ways. For example, when the Italians took offense at pious Pope Adrian VI (and not just because of his well-known piety, which would be an offensive characteristic in a pope!), they made life impossible for him because he was not an Italian. They simply looked upon him as an intruder.

This national feeling erupted in a much more charming and direct manner when the great Humanist Erasmus traveled from Germany to Basel. The enthusiasm, the most generous and most cordial ever accorded him, startled and astonished him, especially since his Humanistic preference attracted him to Paris and even more to Oxford. And perhaps the good Germans—so easily enthused—themselves sensed in their dullness that Erasmus was really only a catalyst who gave impetus to their national spirit. Later on the right man was to come: Luther. The sources of German history were rediscovered, particularly the *Germania* by Tacitus; and an extravagantly patriotic book, the new *Germania,* came from the pen of Wimpfeling, the Alsatian Humanist.

But all this was only a beginning.

There was, however, one area in which the awakening of the nations was more than a mere beginning: the area of the religious faith. Before this most vital phase of these days can be discussed, we must attempt a brief survey of the intellectual world at that time.

The Intellectual Scene

The intellectual world experienced changes unparalleled in western civilization. Literally, a new world hove into view, the New World discovered by *Columbus.*

This young, imaginative Genoese found no sympathy for his plans among his countrymen and was finally equipped by the Spanish crown with the caravel "Santa Maria," which today looks like a nutshell in comparison to modern ocean liners. This man, in whom a modern and almost Faustian "yearning for the vast distances" was combined with a profound medieval mysticism, is a symbol of the collision of the two eras. He was inspired to venture on his journey by the handbook of geography written by the great Parisian Scholastic, Pierre d'Ailly, one of the most outstanding theologians of his day, and one to whom Luther was also greatly indebted. When Columbus embarked on that adventurous journey, which was supposed to take him to the East Indies but instead took him to the West Indies, he took along with him another book, a lovely and profound treatise, filled with pious meditations, by the same author, the man who had played a decisive part in the condemnation of Huss! Thus in the person of Columbus is reflected the spectrum of the most varied strivings reaching out from the Middle Ages to the new age. And now, due to his discovery, a transformation took place in the world view. As a devout member of the medieval church he gave Christian names to the places discovered by him as did those who came after him: Corpus Christi Bay, San Salvador, Santa Maria de la Conception, and others. But behind this Christian veil lurked the ugliest and most cruel form of colonial policy. The Spanish and Portuguese *conquistadores* arrived in large numbers. In contrast to the crusaders before them, however, they no longer illumined Europe with a new, otherworldly glow. Now the undisguised mania for conquest with all its attendant horrors came to the surface. The first colonies were also witnesses to the first colonial brutality.

The money began to flow. The influx of precious metals from the New World (which in the course of the sixteenth century was to attain dizzying levels) added vigor to the economy of the Spanish state. In an economic sense Spain became the strongest power, but simultaneously the old curse that comes with gold was invoked. Spain could endure this wealth for no more than a century. An increasingly acute economic crisis engulfed all of Europe from the middle of the sixteenth century on.

However, the new, broader, wider view of the world revealed unlimited horizons which no longer terrified man nor inspired in him a boundless sense of awe. Sober and resolute views were fixed not only on the new west, but also upon the frontiers in the east: the northern coast of Africa and later on the eastern portion of the Mediterranean became the battlegrounds for the great struggles against the growing Turkish menace, and some of the most brilliant victories of this century buttressed the conviction that man was still the master of his world.

All this took place in a world whose pattern of life was still decidely medieval in character. Every kind of superstition was still widely rampant, and even Columbus became its victim.

Thus the attention of the world was once again directed toward its perimeters. For the first time since the crusades an expansionist urge, which had been practically alien to medieval man, once again asserted itself. The Faustian era began, and the Faustian restlessness became man's master. Astronomers dared to blaze new trails; inventors appeared on the scene. Their work was primitive, yet it was destined to effect a fundamental change in man's picture of the world.

This change was much more evident in the *intellectual world* than in that of politics and geography.

There was *Erasmus,* the prince of Humanists. This blond Hollander, of more than average height, with white skin and florid complexion, and the keen face of a thinker, was in more than one respect the apex of Humanism. He had gone beyond merely imitating the ancients and had himself restored Latin as a truly living language. His collection of proverbs, the *Adagia,* was a first-rate publication success which made available to the people of average education a useful compendium and introduction to the world of antiquity. His *Colloquies* were masterpieces of journalism—orderly, cultured, and intellectually significant. These essays were for his day what the editorials of a leading newspaper would be today. Their influence, however, was incomparably greater since they had not yet become a threadbare medium for influencing public opinion, and because they were on an eminently high intellectual level. The most significant thing about these essays was the easy candor with which he, who certainly desired to be a faithful member of the church, attacked the thinking of the Middle Ages, even that of the church. He dealt with relics and pilgrimages with such superior and deadly ridicule that not even Luther could have produced anything more caustic. His efforts to contemporize Christian doctrine were such that at more than one point he shattered the medieval conception of the world. In one of his Oxford conversations, when his turn came to speak at the round table of the Humanists, he told the story of the angel with drawn sword who stands guard at the gates of Paradise. One of the persons in the dialogue shouted up to the angel: "You there! Why are you still standing around up there with that ridiculous thing? Are you still guarding the gate? Down here we've been using dogs for that!" He continued by combining the Prometheus legend of man's rebellion against the gods with the biblical story of the fall in such a clever manner that the essential difference between the two was no longer recognizable. This dazzling ambiguity is characteristic of the spirit which pervaded the entire intellectual approach of that epoch. As Burckhardt said in his *Humanitas Christiana:* "All the intellectual heavens were newly oriented."

Art, the most sensitive guage of the life of the spirit, offered proof of Burckhardt's statement. The exquisite gold background in the pictures of the Siena saints which had lifted these figures above the earthly turmoil and radiantly transfigured them was now gone. It was replaced by airy blue landscapes with long vistas toward rivers and valleys. The figures were set free from the hierarchical postures of liturgical scenes; now there was movement in the folds of saintly robes and life in facial expressions. Man stepped to the fore as he really was. This became even clearer in the case of sculptures: the figures were detached from the shadows of the pillars and vaulted portals of the Gothic cathedrals and stepped forth as real human beings of flesh and blood. The elongated sculptures of the Gothic saints that, with their celestial softness and their ecstatic prayer gestures, had blended so magnificently with the heaven-directed maze of columns and flying buttresses of the Gothic cathedral, now gave way to sculptured figures which breathed the newly discovered immediacy of life recovered by the Renaissance's look backward to antiquity.

This transition cannot be recorded by precise dates on the pages of a calendar. The old world did not simply yield to the new; the two worlds collided and intermingled, just as a mighty river conjoins with the one into which it flows. *Jerome Bosch,* who painted at the turn of the century can be cited as an example. In his famous painting *Garden of Lusts,* which today can be seen in the Prado, he depicts the host of demons who beset the human senses. The picture is crowded with sinister creatures. All kinds of evil spirits roam about freely: there is the Ear, addicted to the sounds of music, pierced by the pinpricks of unending music; there is a little heap of a man, glued to a harp from which he cannot free himself; there are the vices of the dice and the hunt as well as the most excessive of all lusts, lasciviousness and gluttony. But in the center of this very medieval embodiment of the lusts one can perceive a pale human face—medieval in character and filled with horror in the face of this world of unleashed demons; but this face is also infinitely "modern," in a human way very akin to us in its awareness of the unfathomable knowledge of this world: man himself, living, suffering man in this Walpurgis Night of medieval excesses.

It is primarily this juxtaposition which is so amazing and also so revealing: Grünewald grips the hand of Dürer who follows him; Breughel takes over from Bosch. This uninterrupted transition is most distinct in the realm of *music:* some of the great melodies of the Middle Ages echoed mightily over into the new era where they were accepted as a normal spiritual and intellectual heritage, but filled with new content and sung with a new fervor. This was especially true of Luther's might hymn "Death surrounds us all through life," in which the forceful medieval *"Media vita in morte sumus"* transmitted one of the profoundest insights of medieval faith to the dawning new day and endowed it with a new dynamic.

But there is still another reason why this change in the intellectual world became so immensely effective. This was the *art of printing,* the importance of which simply cannot be exaggerated. Of course, the later publishing business and our present-day techniques for the distribution of literature were just beginning. Printers were also publishers and they printed whatever they found or wherever they could locate something suitable. The idea of the copyright did not exist; there was no protection against reprints being made, and only a few people looked upon this reprinting as shameful or commercially unfair. Luther, for example, never received a penny for his prodigious literary production, which was by far the most extensive of his day. On the contrary, however, his printer at Wittenberg was able to build himself a very handsome house from the profits on these writings. But the public effectiveness of the art of printing was all the greater. In fact, the leaflets, brochures, and books of these centuries generated that modern phenomenon which we call "public opinion." The almost fantastic influence of Erasmus, his popularization of antiquity in the best sense, and the dissemination of his reform polemics among the broad masses of the people presupposed the existence of the printing press. Erasmus looked upon this potential for the expansion of influence as being one of the greatest advantages of his time. He felt the way people later did when they recognized the immense commercial and advertisement possibilities inherent in radio broadcasting.

The simple prerequisite for the realization of Erasmus' ideal was the printing press. If, for example, it was his desire to place the New Testament into the hands of every person, as he stated in one of his finest and most often cited passages, then this was conceivable only at a time when the possession of a Bible was no longer dependent on a personal fortune, when a copy could be purchased at a cost within everyone's reach. The fact that there was such a thing as public opinion was significant not only for the world of religion, but also for other branches of public life such as politics and economics. Although public opinion did not carry much weight politically, it still exerted a certain amount of influence. As the princes and the pope learned only too well, public opinion played an important role during the sixteenth century in spiritual matters, which then as now and always were fundamental and urgent drives. The Reformation would have been quite inconceivable without this new technique for the dissemination of spiritual insights. The densely populated cities were especially ideal seedbeds of public opinion. It was true not only in communal but also in intellectual matters that city air had a liberating influence. It was not by chance that the free and independent imperial cities played such a vital role within the Reformation movement. They not only possessed the power to mold public opinion, they also championed it.

Luther, however, was the first to raise the new invention to the level of highest efficiency. In those days and as a result of the art of printing, public opinion was almost totally subject to the influence of a single person.

The Ecclesiastical Scene

Externally the church offered an amazing picture. The pope was the visible representative of the church and at no other time did the visual manifestation of the church count for so much as then. A curious and very complex line of popes occupied the throne of Peter during this period. But in order to do justice to them as we subject them to our detailed scrutiny, we must first give some attention to the situation of the papacy in general.

Since the middle of the fifteenth century the popes were virtually nothing but secular princes. And that was still about the best that one could say about them. The marvelous exhileration of the Renaissance had taken hold of Rome, and the free, unfettered worldliness of the art of antiquity set the style in the papal palaces, life at the papal court, and public life in general. Unfortunately, this new epoch included not only poets and sculptors, painters and architects, but also poison, murder, jealousy, greed, inordinate excesses, and lust for power. The most outstanding characteristic of the papacy during the Renaissance was its nonchalant conduct. We have one of the worst popes to thank for the Sistine Chapel. In his amazing dual capacity as a patron of the arts and as a scoundrel, this pope has immortalized his name. This moral insensibility occasionally had its grandiose aspects. Alexander VI, a Borgia, a Spaniard, and the last of a line of notoriously wicked popes, nephew of Callistus III whose nepotism brought him ill fame, appeared on the balcony of his papal palace with his arm placed about his daughter as they admired the stud horses from his farm. He was a virile, handsome child of nature, and his face betrayed the unyielding firmness and clarity of the race from which he was descended. More recent research has virtually established the fact that he died of the very poison which he had intended for someone else. In this vicar of Christ the desire for revenge was a vital part of his being.

A similar personality, Julius II, stood at the beginning of the new century. Probably echoing Erasmus, Luther called him simply the "blood-bibber," or "the old lion with the white mane." The people of his day were unanimous in their resentment at the many bloody wars which he personally conducted. This resentment is illustrated by one of the most rancorous writings of this era: *Julius exclusus* ("Julius, who has been barred from heaven"), a clever Humanistic dialogue in which the pope, his bloodstained armor concealed by his papal vestments, vainly seeks entrance at the portals of heaven. Saint Peter, however, refuses to admit this blooddrenched figure. An attempt can be made to do Julius justice: like Machiavelli he recognized that Italy's basic problem was that of its division into many territories. He conscientiously did his best to forge a unity based on a formula which later proved to be so effective and which did full honor to his historic and political sagacity: the formula of blood and iron. Yet it could not be overlooked that in such plans he went far beyond the actual realm of duties incumbent upon him in his lofty Christian office! Though they were inured to the bloody wars of their rulers, his contemporaries certainly bore him strong personal resentment because he was unable to differentiate between his armor and his tiara. This judgment reflects one of the most profound changes taking place in those days. Until now it had been only such spiritually-minded souls as the austere and brave successors of Francis of Assisi and other apostles of "inwardness" who had viewed this papal witches' sabbath of murderous poisonings, licentiousness, and the welter of worldly ways during the preceding century as an abomination, whereas Christians as a whole tolerated this corruption with a strange patience. All this was now changed.

In the sixteenth century the Borgias were succeeded by the Medici, an upcoming family of bankers whose wealth soon reached such vast proportions that there was no reason not to rank them among the royal families of Europe. In their own fashion, two women from this royal house graced the throne of France during the sixteenth and seventeenth centuries. The Medici popes were all princes of culture, adept in the art of political finesse, although with varying degrees of success. Leo X, the pope in Luther's time, showed a willingness to arrange for a settlement of the unpleasant, tumultuous dispute in Germany by means of polished diplomacy. His nephew was Julius Medici, who served him first as papal secretary of state and who later became Pope Clement VII. He fell heir to a difficult political situation: the papacy faced financial bankruptcy; there was imminent danger that he would be ground to bits between the two millstones of France and Hapsburg. During his reign the Eternal City was subjected to its worst trial, the sacking of Rome in the year 1527, when a revolt of the lansquenets swept down upon Rome and wreaked unimaginable havoc there. On top of this the marital affair of Henry VIII reached its climax during his pontificate. It was a hardship for Clement to sustain so many losses at one time, especially since the marriage problem became the external pretext for Henry to separate the Church of England from Rome. It should be added that those historians who praise Clement in this instance because he supposedly adhered so loyally to papal principles are guilty of misrepresentation. In other even more troublesome cases the papacy had managed to find a loophole and had not been inconvenienced by its principles. The decisive factor in the case of Henry lay in the fact that in the political power play Charles V, the nephew of Henry's wife, carried more weight than did Henry. Clement is simply an insignificant pope who is presented with the bill for a papal policy which long ago had deviated from the true mission of the papacy. Ranke and Pastor have called his pontificate the "most fateful in the history of the popes." His perfidy and unreliability toward Charles contributed not a little to the fact that the princes loyal to the Reformation had a free hand. Perhaps the greatest harm was done by his tenacious and quiet opposition to a council of the church. He was a bad pope. That which in the case of Julius II gave the impression of strength, was in his case twisted into weakness. The papacy had turned itself into a fully secular power. But Italy, whose political factionalism Julius II had been unable to overcome, was not the right soil for such secular power aspirations, and since the papacy was lacking in the decisive ownership of lands, this particular approach could result in only a very modest existence. In Italy the papacy became a third rate territorial power, the plaything of the nations contending for control of Italy. And no matter how many diplomatic threads were spun by the Curia, and no matter how much the Curia was involved in intrigue—if Ranke is correct—this fate still could not be avoided. It is said that the pope seriously considered the possibility of entering into an alliance with Francis I and the Turks against Charles.

As in the case of Julius II, the external political mission which the papacy had chosen for itself could not be fulfilled. The pope had to wear either the tiara or armor, but not the one on top of the other. If the papacy wanted to continue playing a part in the political games of the world (and this intention was very evident), then it had to substitute the art of diplomatic strategy for its nonexistent institutional authority. The papacy later learned this lesson when Consalvi, papal secretary of state at the time of the Congress of Vienna, managed to play a role as spokesman of the papacy equal to that of Tallyrand and Metternich, even though Napoleon had just previously inflicted shameful humiliation on the papacy.

Between these Medici and the other Italians, like an omen of future papal renewal, there stood the strangely lonely and engaging figure of Adrian VI of Holland. He had been the childhood tutor of Charles V. Adrian's imperial master had such confidence in him that he later sent him to Spain on important political assignments, and finally the emperor chose him to be pope. But he turned out to be a strange kind of a pope, not at all like an Italian *capitano*, or like one of the Renaissance princes addicted to the enjoyment of the sophisticated life. He was a pope who at the Diet of Nürnberg (1522-1523) began with a confession of sins in behalf of the church! Thus he was a dangerous pope because he took things seriously. The question still persists whether the Reformation would have culminated in a break with Rome if in its early, crucial years this man, so fervent in faith and so determined in behalf of all that is holy, had been seated on the throne of St. Peter. But at this time a pope who was primarily and seriously concerned with the church and his Christian office was still an unusual phenomenon in Rome. An early death released him from his bitter and hopeless situation. The very lovely monument above his tomb, erected in his honor in the German Catholic Church of Santa Maria dell' Anima at Rome, symbolizes his high-minded but fruitless life's work: his left hand supports the noble head, seemingly too weary to bear the burden of the tiara and now overpowered by the sleep of death. Now the papal policy of the Medici again returned to claim its rights.

Adrian was just an interlude, but this interlude made it abundantly clear that the renewal of the church could not originate within the papacy. In the overall picture of the papacy of that period the brief appearance of Adrian VI is without any significance whatever. There was no room for the penitential earnestness of this man in a city like Rome where, in the words of Burckhardt, the basic characteristic was that of a "magnificent cheerfulness." It is nevertheless amazing that lovely, great, majestic, and worldly

Rome was able to maintain and enhance itself amidst the martial turmoils of the times. But the church could be saved only by other persons. Ignatius of Loyola, the austere, ascetic Basque, the army officer and mystic, became the field commander who reconquered Europe for the church. The popes would never have been able to do this.

In their own way the popes and cardinals were cultured and significant personalities. When Julius II died, still energetic although almost a septuagenarian, he completed a life full of ambitious military and political plans. He was a realistic politician of considerable stature with an almost modern unscrupulousness about his methods—but he simply was not a pope. The same princes of the church who a century before had condemned John Huss at Constance spent the days when the council was not in session by scouring the neighborhood for valuable old manuscripts and succeeded in bringing treasures from the monasteries of St. Gallen, Reichenau, and Ufenau to Rome.

But whoever penetrated the visible outer facade of papal policy and became acquainted with the financial dealings of the Curia—and this can be said for more than a few contemporaries—could not refrain from wondering what all this worldly bustle might have in common with being a follower of Him who while on earth had "not where to lay his head."

The papacy itself had depleted what residue of spiritual authority it still had. More than once the western world had witnessed the rivalry of two or even three contending popes. Such scandal jeopardized the Christian unity of the west. By becoming progressively more casual in their unrestricted use of the church's spiritual authority and discipline, the popes undermined the effectiveness of their anathemas and interdicts until these penalties lost their meaning. Even the most simple-minded and trusting Christian was bound to be perplexed when Pius II declared it a mortal sin—for which no indulgence was available—for a person to withhold revenues by not patronizing the alum depositories at Tolfa which were a papal monopoly! Originally, excommunication from the congregation of believers and the interdict against participation in all churchly rites had been spiritual measures; if now the papacy itself was instrumental in divesting these measures of their meaning, their effectiveness was inevitably gone.

A reaction was bound to set in. It is frightening and distressing to note the casualness with which the contemporaries took the spiritual criticism leveled against the papacy. The need for a "reform in head and members" was considered to be so pressing and normal that no one defended the present state of the papacy.

Similar severe losses had been sustained by another institution which had once supplied the papal church with its most courageous, selfless, and successful vanguard: *monasticism*. Even though the church of the thirteenth century was indebted to the mendicant orders for a kind of renewal and though it was they who served the church extremely well in the cities and among the mass movements which arose during the peak of the Middle Ages, it was these orders which deteriorated most. The ideal of poverty which St. Francis had preached had turned into mendicancy, and mendicancy into laziness. In the meantime, the immorality of the Franciscans had become proverbial. Erasmus heaped sarcastic ridicule on their lack of self-discipline and on the dullness of the abbots. It seems that the great commission which had inspired monkhood since the days of Benedict of Nursia was forgotten. The eyes of the world were fixed not upon the devout and earnest people behind cloistered walls but upon those who were unworthy.

It is truly touching to see how the *piety of the common people* searched for avenues of expression other than monasticism. Outwardly they walked every step of the unspiritual road that leads to extreme forms of superstition. The magical and mechanical means of piety—relics, indulgences, and pilgrimages—had an uncanny hold over them. In the *Colloquies* of Erasmus one can read a critique of them that is candid and intellectually excellent, but which is also tinged with religious piety. But of what avail was a brilliant Humanistic critique when pitted against a fact that was more influential than all argumentation, namely, medieval man's terrible fear of death, purgatory, and the tortures of hell! And this world, in which each person had to endure death, was his very own world. The never-ending crusades dragged in their wake not only vast numbers of lansquenets, but affected the countries involved. Added to this was the helplessness in the face of numerous epidemics which broke out repeatedly and swept through the populous cities because of their abysmal sanitary conditions. Unless a person of this era was a member of the small, select circle of rulers and intellectual aristocrats, the truth of the hymn "In the midst of life we are in death," was as much a part of his life as his daily bread.

As a result, all those who were able to offer the common man comfort in the hour of his death, exerted the strongest influence on him. One of the very loveliest comforters is the treasured booklet *The Imitation of Christ*, attributed to the pen of Thomas a Kempis, a quiet, beatific man from the monastery of Mount St. Agnes near Zwolle. In the midst of the witches' brew of the corrupt papal church, and surrounded by the brilliant but always uncommitted criticisms of the Humanists, this dialogue between the exalted Lord and his follower sounds like a wondrously soft devotional melody which helps us forget the noise made by others. This valuable little treatise, which Luther highly esteemed, was the Bible of the people. But that which constituted its content was also a living force on other pages and in other places: gentle hymns of praise sung by seeking souls ring through the confusing welter of sounds that characterize the Middle Ages. Although the glamorous world of kings and prelates emits other kinds of sounds, the adoration of God and his grace was never fully muted.

In order to complete the picture of the Middle Ages it is also necessary to take a look at its *theology*. In addition to being one of the most impressive accomplishments of this era, theology also represents one of the very outstanding stylistic forms of the Middle Ages. Its attainments in the world of ideas, the tremendous system of thought in which the philosophy of the Middle Ages was summarized, are worthy counterparts to the imposing cathedrals erected during those centuries. What Gothic was to architecture, Scholasticism was not only to theology but to the entire intellectual life of the western world.

It is not easy to elucidate medieval theology for the nontheologian in just a few sentences. Perhaps the best way to explain this theology is to proceed historically.

The basis of medieval theology was the impressive system of thought constructed by Thomas Aquinas. His chief works all bear the title *Summa*. He gave expression to the intellectual conclusions reached by his age. He took the total world view of his day as it had been molded by the rediscovery of Aristotle, and with his unusual reasoning powers placed that world view in the service of the church. Through the Arab invasions the submerged world of the Greeks—their philosophy and natural science, their mathematics and astronomy—had again become a vital intellectual factor and confronted the world of traditional Christian ideas. Scholasticism met the challenge of this confrontation, and one of the most definitive and effective intellectual works to emerge was that of Thomas Aquinas. The intellectual and theological labors of the following centuries continued to build diligently on the groundwork of his lucid, compact thought structure.

The reader who knows something about the importance of Thomistic theology for contemporary Catholicism, must, however, be made aware of a remarkable difference. Since 1879, when Leo XIII pronounced the teachings of St. Thomas as the guide and rule of Catholic theology and thereby bound up all the dogmatic labors of Catholic research to Thomas, the philosophy of Thomas—through Neo-Thomism—has exercised a predominant influence in the intellectual activity of modern Catholicism. Frequently this intellectual activity consists of nothing more than an exposition of Thomas. Even brilliant Catholic thinkers, whose work is characterized by precision of thought as well as earnest religiousness, follow this procedure: on the basis of an ofttimes very intelligent examination of a subject, the basic results of an investigation are traced back to a formula, the answer to which is found with relative ease in the philosophical system of St. Thomas. Strange as it may seem, the late Middle Ages had a decidely freer and less committed attitude toward Thomas. This was not the case simply because he did not as yet enjoy that status of exclusive authority conferred upon him by the decree of Leo XIII, but also because the intellectual activities of Scholasticism were still very much in a state of flux.

It is significant that it was two Anglo-Saxons who were not satisfied with the polished unity of Thomas' achievements: Duns Scotus and William of Occam. An almost modern atmosphere pervades their ideas. In contrast to the carefully reasoned, intellectual confidence of Thomas, in whose work *all* questions are answered from the vantage point of faith, these two men are more skeptical about the capability of human reason to perceive the truth. It does not lie in our power to decide with certainty whether the concepts *(nomina)* which we have established, always correspond fully to the reality which they are supposed to express. We must content ourselves with the limitations set for us by our comprehension of reality. This is never more true than when we are speaking about God. For these Anglo-Saxon thinkers and their followers it is virtually a sign of our reverence toward God's revelation that man should not attempt to state more about that revelation than he is permitted to do. It was this revision and limitation of Thomistic theology which particularly preoccupied the century preceding the Reformation.

The two most typical spokesmen of this new thought trend were prominent figures at the Council of Constance: Pierre d'Ailly and John Gerson. The memory of the council which sent John Huss to the stake becomes doubly painful and embarrassing when one realizes that his condemnation was brought about by the leadership of these two men who were among the most cultured and progressive theologians of their day. They were already fully under the influence of the other dynamic movement— *Humanism*—which brought about the end of medieval theology. Although Humanism was more than a theological movement, its most powerful and penetrating influence was exerted in the field of theology.

At this point we must again speak about Erasmus, for it was he who most clearly embodied the theological attainments of Humanism. His oftmentioned failings have tended to relegate his very substantial accomplishments into the background, and we ought to contribute something toward the restoration of his good name. For even though many are still unwilling to forgive him for not being what Luther became, one ought nevertheless not lose sight of the fact that among the Humanists he was the most mature in his theology and the most morally virtuous of Christians. He was motivated by a basic yearning for purity, peace, and order. This profound longing was the basis of his extensive labors which made him the intellectual leader of his generation: namely, his intelligent critique of the abuses existing in the church, through which he opened the door to the Reformation; and his theological work, above all the textual editions, of which the publication of the New Testament in Greek of 1516 was the most important. In 1505, with his reputation as a Humanist established, he published Lorenzo Valla's *Annotations on the New Testament*. In 1516 in Basel he published the first Greek edition of the New Testament together with a methodologically important introduction about the nature and purpose of true theology. This publication did not do credit to Erasmus as a scholar, for he produced it in inexcusable haste and levity, and he himself admitted that the edition was "more ejected than edited." But in his favor we must not forget that in this area he did more spadework for the Reformation than did others among his contemporaries. The things he said about the reading of the Scriptures, about its authority and significance for temporal and eternal life, rank among the most significant utterances made by anyone in the time prior to Luther.

But it was not without reason that this towering spirit died lonely and embittered, even though at about the time Luther posted his *Ninety-five Theses* he was enjoying universal fame. History, which he had shared in fashioning as had no other mind of his era, may not have rolled over him, but it did storm past him. He shared the fate of many brilliant diagnosticians: the fundamental decisions were not made by him. His tremendous intellectual potential was ground to pieces between the papacy, which he had attacked with caustic satire but which he was unable to renounce, and Luther's Reformation, for which his intellectual activity had blazed a trail, but to which he did not dare to commit himself unequivocally.

The significance of the total theological effort of this period is that it raised all of the issues to which the era of the Reformation gave answers. The universal restlessness of this century was reflected in its theology. The widespread yearning for a "reformation in head and members" came to life in all its issues—in its critical attitude toward the papacy, the monastic ideals of piety, and the matter of indulgences. Almost all the questions had now been formulated. Christendom awaited the answer.

Woodcut of the dream of
Frederick the Wise at Schweinitz in 1517,
also mentioned by Luther in his *Table Talk*.

The Upheaval

To modern men the cupola of St. Peter's that rises above the skyline of the city of Rome symbolizes the centrality of Rome in the world during the periods of antiquity, the Middle Ages, and the modern era. The edifice which stood on this site before the present cathedral assuredly had a venerable history, dating back to the time of Emperor Constantine the Great. However, toward the end of the Middle Ages it did not conform to the prevailing concepts of what the main apostolic sanctuary of the universal Roman church should be like. Thus, under Nicholas V (1447-1455), plans for the rebuilding of St. Peter's were initiated; actual construction began during the pontificate of Julius II (1503-1513). The demolition and reconstruction of the old church of the apostle symbolized the upheaval and renewal within the church. The sketch by the Dutch artist Maarten van Heemskerk gives a graphic view of the new pillars and vaults rising up in the midst of the old building that is being razed. The new pillars and vaults will support the cupola designed later on by Michelangelo.

Demolition of old St. Peter's Church, by Maarten van Heemskerk.

The Church of That Day

Since its beginnings in Roman times about the year 67 A.D. (following the martyrdom of the apostles Peter and Paul), through the times of the great migrations of peoples and later antiquity, the papacy and the church had developed and perpetuated themselves up to the early and main Middle Ages as those institutions of the western world which through the centuries had played the decisive role in molding the spirit and the external history of the west.

There was hardly a single aspect or area of human life that did not have some contextual relationship to the church. The state, in our modern sense of a regulatory power, did not exist as yet. Important functions of society such as culture and educational systems on the higher and lower levels, the promotion of the sciences, the entire welfare and health program for the infirm, the invalid, the aged—all were in the hands of the church. These projects were financed by gifts and bequests to the church and by its vast estates. In fact, in areas under the control of archbishops and bishops, secular and ecclesiastical powers were frequently united in one person; the same was true in the sovereign estates of the large monasteries and abbeys. Not to be overlooked are those lands later on designated by the pope as church-states.

Everything was embraced within a uniform, Christian world view. This world view was hierarchical in its structure, stratified according to class, embraced heaven and earth, and started with the lowly peasants and poor folk and culminated in the pope as the vicar of Christ on earth. It was unthinkable for an emotion or an idea or a human experience to exist apart from God's sovereignty, the redemptive act of Christ, or the papal power of the keys. Insofar as it was a human affair, tensions within this structure were inevitable and did occur, but the institutional edifice remained intact for many centuries.

A change took place toward the end of the Middle Ages. Generations of people were born who, unconsciously at first, but then with an ever-growing intensity, pressed for a restructuring of things. Not only the state, but the individual as well, proclaimed his autonomy. Both discovered their basic independence and demanded recognition and rights outside the hitherto existent order and Christian standards. Both based their claims on phenomena which until then had been judged as lying outside the Christian world, namely, the world of antiquity and its pagan view of life, and on the concept of man as they had lived and experienced it.

People began to rediscover all this in the literature, the arts, the philosophy, the political theories, and the history of the ancients—matters which during the Middle Ages were never completely unknown, but which, as far as the general awareness was concerned, had been buried. This pagan world view was now resurrected in a kind of rebirth—a Renaissance, as it was called—and one frequently failed to distinguish what was an originally pagan value from that which had its source in a new vitality and a new experience of life.

Beginning about 1350 (the middle of the life of the poet Petrarch), all this took place in Italy as a partly evolutionary, partly revolutionary process that left hardly a single area of life untouched.

In other countries of Europe, and especially in Germany, these phenomena appeared later and in a different form. But everywhere the central theme of the Renaissance remained the same. Institutions, powers, and ideas developed which threatened to shatter or actually did shatter the old world order. Inasmuch as these processes were expressed most directly and most violently in Italy, the papacy as the hierarchical summit was also drawn into this cataclysm and the entire structure of the church was affected by it.

"It is an article of faith that there is a church. Therefore we must grasp the church in faith, not see it with our eyes. To do this God has hidden the church by wondrous means: sometimes by sins, sometimes by schisms and false doctrine, sometimes by weakness, offenses, death of the pious and increase of the godless, etc. He was so eager to have this concealment, that he even deemed the conflict between the apostles to be necessary, as seen in the struggle of Paul against Peter, or in the differences of opinion between Mark, Barnabas, and Paul. And it is required of us to believe that all of Asia, which has become famous through so many great names, defected from Paul for no other reason than that thereby the church might be hidden. For there certainly had been a church in Asia, even though among very few people who were known to God alone."

Luther's *Table Talk*

Ruler and Priest

As spiritual head of the church Pope Julius II
had begun the reconstruction of St. Peter's
cathedral, but as the secular ruler of the
church-state he had, by military ventures and
diplomatic maneuvers, also regained all lands
which in the preceding centuries had been lost
to the church. He proved himself a master in all
those practices and endeavors which in the Italy
of this period created what we call the modern
power state. The Vatican, which Bramante
expanded for him to become the largest palatial
structure in the world, was replete with worldly
splendor, urbane life and courtly pleasures.
A contemporary engraving of a tournament in
the Court of St. Damaso shows this vividly.
Above the roof of the palace to the right, towers
the still unfinished drum of the cupola of St. Peter's.

The great tournament in the Court of St. Damaso
at the Vatican, by Jacob Bink.

47

The Giant

After centuries of being oriented toward the supernatural, men were now led by the rediscovery of antiquity to the cult of the human being and to unfettered abandon to the delirious enjoyment of this world. It is true that St. Peter's Church was constructed in praise of God. However, it was not as an escape from this world but with the objective of manifesting God in the splendors of earthly existence that motivated Julius II to surround himself with the most prominent artists of his day. He did this in order to proclaim God and the church of God, and to immortalize himself as the ancients did and thereby to win fame for all ages to come. This was the intent of his tomb for which he commissioned Michelangelo.

Michelangelo's Moses, erected on the tomb of Julius II in the Church of S. Pietro in Vinculi at Rome.

Julius II, chrome woodcut by Hans Burgkmair.

The Pope in Armor

*Julius II, who occupied St. Peter's throne during the years
that Luther spent in the monastery and prior to the posting
of the Theses, is characterized better by his martial
undertakings than by his role as a patron. He symbolizes
the secularization of the church. In 1506 he waged war
against Perugia and Bologna, in 1509 against Venice, in 1511
and 1512 against France. His alliances with the major
powers of his day reveal his attempt to pave the way for an
Italy free of foreign influence. In his day he was the
embodiment of the Italian national consciousness.*

Leo X, drawing by
Sebastiano del Piombo.

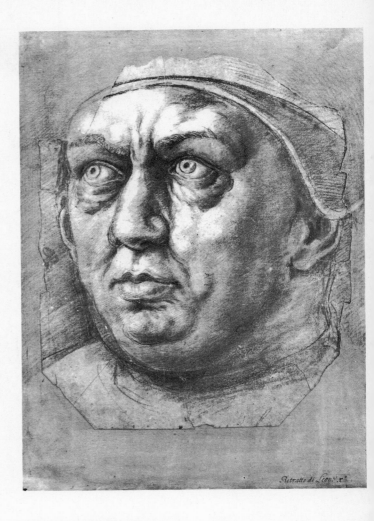

Aesthete and
Man of the World

*Leo X reigned as pope during the critical years of the Reformation
between 1517 and 1521. He was motivated by worldly interests
and amusements even more than his predecessors. Innocent VIII
made him a cardinal when he was fourteen years old. When
elected to the papacy he was a cardinal-deacon and had been
neither ordained to the priesthood nor consecrated a bishop.
In the realm of politics he was interested in compromise and
peace, but merged the interests of the church-state with those
of Florence. He was always in financial straits. The
indulgence dispute interested him only insofar as the question
of money was involved. He had absolutely no understanding
of the religious problems which he himself had stirred up.*

Adrian VI,
by Jan van Scorel.

The Powerless Confessor

*What Leo X had tried by all means to prevent, finally happened
in 1519: Charles I of Spain became German Emperor
Charles V. The powers of Spain and the empire, now united
in one hand, flanked the church-state in the north as well as in the
south. The influence of Charles V was evident at the conclave
of 1522. He chose as the new pope his former tutor,
Adrian Dedel, Grand Inquisitor and the king's regent in Spain:
Adrian VI. His pontificate started out initially with moves in
the direction of reforming the church, but an early death in 1523
put an end to his endeavors. However, he bequeathed to
posterity a solemn admission of the Curia's share of guilt for
the schism within the church.*

Mockery of monasticism, an allegorical woodcut by H. S. Beham.

The Decline of Morality

*At the end of the medieval period monasticism, without which
life and the cultural accomplishments of the Middle Ages are
unthinkable, deteriorated to the same degree in which it had
once been exemplary and respected. It was reproached for every
possible vice, from drunkenness to adultery and to the
frequenting of brothels. A tremendous contempt for the orders
and the mendicants found expression in words and pictures.*

Religious Fervor

*The more the thought-world of the late Middle Ages became
agitated and the more directly the real world invaded the place
where man was, so much the more was his daily existence subject
to intolerable tensions: ecstatic joys of life alternated abruptly
with a mystical withdrawal from the world, and gaudy ostentation
with scenes of dolorous seclusion. A typical example of a
sudden blaze of mass hysteria was the rapturous pilgrimage*

Pilgrimage to the shrine of the Beautiful Madonna of Regensburg, by Michael Ostendorfer.

to the Beautiful Madonna of Regensburg, which is depicted in
a woodcut by Michael Ostendorfer. Wolfgang Marius, abbot
of the Cistercian monastery at Aldersbach, describes it in these
words: "Boys, young men, girls, mothers, and men came to
this place as if they were possessed. . . . If they happened to
have a tool or implement in their hands they brought it along.
None, however, carried a knapsack. They were in such a
hurry that many of them arrived half naked, bereft of voice and
senses, totally exhausted after running day and night without
food or drink. . . . When they reached the place, most of them
would fall sobbing to the ground, as though in a state of
ecstasy. . . . Rising again after a long time they found themselves
thrown upon the mercy of the local citizens who were at pains
to recall them to their senses and to send them back to their
homes. After they had regained consciousness and departed for
their homes, one could see on the plaza in front of the merciful
statue so many purses and other articles that one could have
filled several wagons with them. This influx of persons so
increased in numbers that many a person preferred to make the
pilgrimage voluntarily lest otherwise he be subjected to
pressures that would force him to come there."

A rosary scene for one of
the indulgence letters of
Pope Alexander VI.

Magic and Mysticism

Simultaneous with the preoccupation with magic, sorcery, and
alchemy, was the pictorialization of the world of religious
and mythical concepts. A powerful impetus was given to these
tendencies by the printing and distribution of woodcuts of
popular pictures. This longing to represent in pictorial form
and to make visible and real to the human eye everything possible—
even the most sublime religious concepts—was overwhelming.
Every aspect of daily life was brought into relationship with one
of the saints and organized in a many-layered system of divine
favors, intercessions, and degrees of merit.

54

55

Emperor
Maximilian
in the year 1518,
a chrome pen
drawing by
Albrecht Dürer.

The Aging Emperor

*Maximilian I, German emperor since 1493, embodied in his weaknesses
and positive features the very essence of his era. He was called "the last of
the knights." Although he was a child of the Renaissance, he preferred
the old way of life. Fighting tenaciously and cunningly for political
advantage, he often appeared to be erratic, undecided, divided within himself.*

The emperor and the estates, drawing from Emperor Maximilian's Autobiography entitled *Weisskunig*, "The White King."

The Rivalry of the Estates

All the emperor's undertakings were paralyzed because of the ambiguity and fragmentation of the law as well as because of inadequate imperial revenues. Although the estates were divided among themselves, they were united in obstructing any kind of imperial reform.

Conventional Weapons

In a time of social ferment within the empire and of the outbreak of wars along all its borders, it was inevitable that such a drastic revolution in the techniques of weapons and methods of warfare as took place on the eve of the Reformation should heighten the restlessness and the insecurity of the masses.

Emperor Maximilian on a visit to the armorer and the ordnance factory, drawings from the *Weisskunig*.

The New Strategy

Emperor Maximilian gave his emphatic support to the newly developing artillery and the new forms of military strategy. He reasoned not as a knight, but as a farsighted army commander who knew that the future belonged to firearms and artillery.

The plundering of
a village,
pen-and-ink drawing
by Hausbuchmeister.

Surrounded
by Enemies

The mentality of the medieval man was both materially concrete and abstractly symbolical. Whenever the tormenting events of daily life were portrayed, it was done against the background of a heaven crowded with mythological creatures and horrible apparitions. In 1495 eternal Public Peace had been proclaimed—but who had the power to enforce it? The feuds continued; merchant caravans were attacked, and villages were plundered. Robber barons, noblemen, and lords thought only of themselves, not realizing that their privileges had become obsolete. The Turkish armies, the enemies of all Christendom, stood at the gates of Europe.

Deployment of the troops during the battles at Vienna-Neustadt against the Turks in 1529, drawing by Michael Ostendorfer from the book *True Description of the Second Campaign in Austria Against the Turks*, printed at Nürnberg MDXXXIX.

60

DER GROS PRACH / LICH HAVFEN

MAGT / LAM

Echerleins angriff

DER BOHMISH RENNFOR

STADT / R. VERTRIBELIN

DER BOHEMISCH RAISIG / ZEVG

DES REICHS GEWALTZI / RAISIG ZEVG

DIE WAGENBVRCK

61

Francis I of France,
by Jean Clouet.

Francis I

*The centralization of power, which could not be achieved in
Germany, was introduced in France by Francis I. The arts were
the beneficiaries of his absolutism. His life was marked by an
unparalleled display of splendor. His four wars against Charles V,
waged without interruption from 1521 to 1546, were the outstanding
events of his reign and served to restrict the emperor's freedom
of movement. Thus his personality is closely interwoven with the
decisive issues of the Reformation.*

Henry VIII of England, by Hans Holbein the Younger.

ANNO · ÆTATIS ·   · SVÆ · XLIX ·

Henry VIII

The reign of Henry VIII of England (1509-1547) coincided roughly with Luther's life from his monastic years to his death. He acknowledged openly and emphatically that he was an enemy of Luther and wrote against him. His defection from Rome in founding the Anglican church was a purely political act. Within the play of major politics that set the emperor and the pope against the Reformation and Francis, Henry's completely England-centered policies were a constant handicap to the emperor and pope in their struggles against the Reformation and Francis.

63

Charles V

During the reign of Maximilian none of the pressing problems of the day were ever truly solved; they were simply postponed. But on the shoulders of Charles V there now rested problems of a basically different kind, fateful for Germany, critical for Europe, and so charged with universal, political import, that a personality of lesser stature would have collapsed. The greatness of this monarch was his moral strength, not his politics, which were destined to be a failure.

Soliman I, the "Magnificent,"
engraving by
Melchior Lorch.

Soliman I

*In 1453 Constantinople had been conquered by the Turks. During the
following decade the entire Balkans fell into their hands. In 1521, at
the climactic moment of the German struggle centered around Luther,
the fall of Belgrade signaled the advance of the Turks under Soliman I
into the heartlands of the empire. As army chieftain, lawgiver, poet,
and potentate, this sultan was one of the most remarkable representatives
of Islam and indeed, of the whole Reformation era. He died in 1566.*

The Terrors of the Times

The art of an era is the most sensitive measure of its spiritual and intellectual condition. Such art demonstrates to us that the late Middle Ages and the early years of the Reformation were times filled with apocalyptic terrors, which manifested themselves in the everyday life of the individual in frightening forms. Religious concepts were concretized in the adoration of the saints and in relics. Added to this was the prevalent belief in witchcraft, the fear of inexplicable natural phenomena, of plagues, famines, and natural catastrophes, intermingled with a sensationalistic mania for miracles and supernatural phenomena. Luther himself, though curbed by constant spiritual self-discipline, serves as the best example of how even in such a person the compulsive forces of fear could lead to unusual apparitions and to extraordinary personal decisions. From his own oft-repeated descriptions we learn how he experienced afflictions and temptations that were very real for him; in fact, they were visible manifestations of the very real world that surrounded him. The grimaces of hell and the devil leered forth from behind the temptations, the everyday tyrannies, and the commonplace daily environment. Surrealism, which today is an art movement with highly intellectual content, yet scarcely part of the existential life of the viewer, at the time of Bosch, Grünewald, Dürer, and all the painters whose works depicted the terrors of their day, represented a true picture of tormented man's fears of death and of the world beyond. These fears were further aggravated and agitated by the language—peppered with threats and crass descriptions of apocalyptic scenes—employed by the preachers, the indulgence salesmen, the authors of tracts and pamphlets, and by all those who might profit from the spiritual anguish of their fellow men. One need only read in the diaries of Albrecht Dürer how even this man, who endeavored to place the stamp of beauty and moderation on his art, was frightened and shaken again and again by the terrors of his day.

The penalties, detail from
The Garden of Lusts by Jerome Bosch.

Temptation

The left wing of the Isenheim altar with the Temptation of St. Anthony *illustrates how very realistically even such an irrational painting must be viewed in all its details. The history of medicine has confirmed that the Order of St. Anthony, which had commissioned Grünewald's painting, was dedicated to the care of those afflicted by the widespread horrible plague called the "Holy Fire" in the homes of incurables owned by the order. The symptoms of this illness are pictured in accurate detail in the figures in the left foreground. On the right wing fourteen plants are depicted that were used in making a medicine to alleviate the debilities of this sickness.*

Temptation of **St. Anthony,** detail from the Isenheim altar by Matthias Grünewald.

The vision, ink sketch by Albrecht Dürer.

Dürer's Dream

Dürer wrote the following (abridged) inscription beneath his water color: "On Tuesday after Pentecost in the year 1525 during the night in my sleep I had this vision of huge torrents of water falling from the skies. The first of these struck the earth about four miles away from me with terrifying dreadfulness, with an overwhelming roar and splash, inundating all the land. The waters came from up so high that it almost seemed as if they were falling slowly. But as they struck the earth, they swelled to such swiftness, with wind and storm, that I was greatly frightened, awoke with my body aquiver, unable for a long time to come to my senses. In the morning I painted the above picture just as I had seen it."

Man Pierces the Celestial Spheres

The miseries, turmoils, and anxieties of the times against which men felt themselves so helpless caused them again and again to seek refuge in a science which gave promise of assuring them insights into cosmic events and the future. They turned to astrology. This was taught at the university on the same level with applied mathematics and astronomy. Luther, though he regarded it as a godless and shabby art, nevertheless spoke of certain planetary constellations as being signs of God.

If, then, the Hellenistic view of the universe as it was espoused by the Middle Ages—with the earth stationary at the center and the spheroidal platters of planets and fixed stars circling it—was so intimately bound up with the life of men and their actions and decisions, then a discovery as revolutionary as that of the movement of the earth and the new insights about the universe resulting from this, were destined to confuse the people of that day.

The spheres and the mechanisms of the heavens, by an unknown artist.

Nicholas Copernicus,
woodcut by an unknown artist.

Scruples and Doubts

*A legend tells us that Nicholas Cusa, the foremost German scholar prior
to the Reformation, whose new insights gave real impetus to our modern
scientific developments, is said to have destroyed the results of his scientific
findings because he was of the opinion that the people of his day were
not mature enough to understand them. Even Copernicus hesitated a
long time before he published his calculations on the movement of the
earth and the stars. He admits that these might appear incredible and
contradict the views held by the masses. Both Copernicus and Cusa, who
were both well versed in the theology and philosophy of their day,
knew that as a consequence of these insights a new day would dawn.
That which was new was bound to destroy the old view of the universe
and its moral standards. In this respect perhaps we who experience
something similar can understand a generation which, like us, was confronted
by a new view of the world fraught with equally grave consequences.*

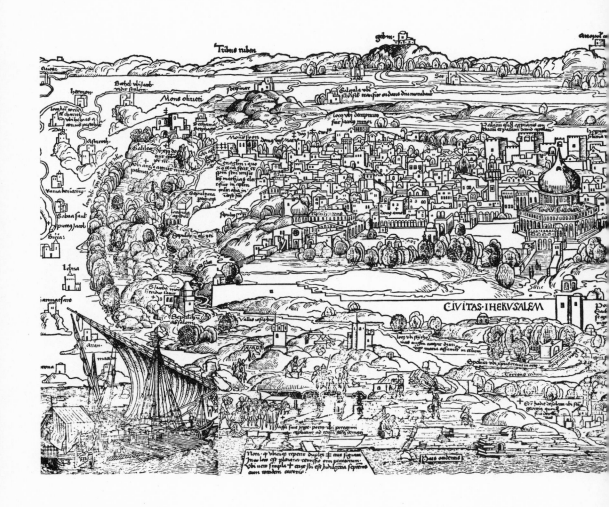

The Old World and the New

During the Middle Ages there were three major sites of pilgrimage: Jerusalem, St. James of Compostela, and Rome. These satisfied the yearnings of many generations for travel, adventure, the wondrous and the exotic. By 1500 the lands involved in the crusades no longer aroused the warlike imagination of the hordes of pilgrims, rather they answered their desire to find edification and peace for their souls.

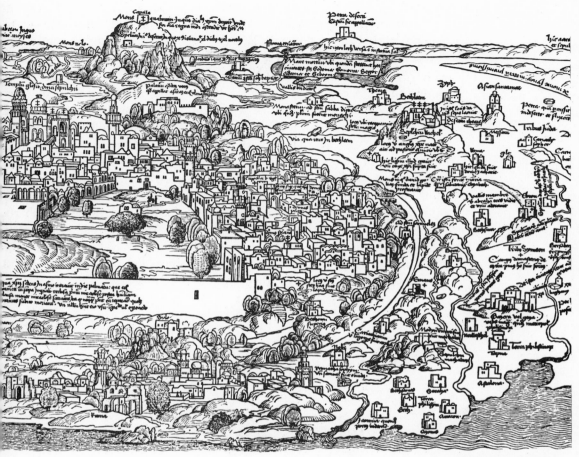

The Holy Land, woodcut by
Bernhard van Breydenbach.

Columbus' caravel, illustration
from the book *De insulis inventis,* printed in Basel in 1494.

All this was changed when on October 12, 1492, Columbus laid eyes on the coast of the New World. When on March 4, 1493, he returned to Europe, a new dimension was added to the outlook of Europeans. The day of discovery and conquest had dawned. Reports from overseas, now widely circulated in the lands of Europe, increased the general unrest of the times. A number of scholars literally did not know how to cope with the new continent, since the writers of antiquity had never mentioned it. But the merchants diligently checked every small detail that could be gleaned about the new "India," since the reports of the discoverers held the promise of new lands, new commercial routes, and new markets. The geographers—especially those in Nürnberg—were proud because they had contributed to the success of Columbus, who on his journey had been equipped with their invention, "the staff of Jacob," and their new charts for the calculation of the position of the stars. When Ulrich von Hutten realized that this world was being revealed to the eyes of his generation in new dimensions of breadth and distance, he burst out in the joyful shout: "O century! It is a joy to be alive!"

Indians (Tiembus), from Schmidel von Straubing.

Erasmus of Rotterdam

He was a scholar who reached the pinnacle of fame in his day. Even among the common people he enjoyed the highest level of popularity. His journey from Holland to Basel in 1521 resembled a triumphal procession. The fate of the sculptured figure shown here may give some indication how effective even a likeness of him was. It was the figure on the stern of the sailing vessel "de Liefde," which traveled to the East Indies. During one such journey this ship ran aground along the coast of Japan. The poop figure was salvaged and acquired by a feudal lord, and since there was something attractive about it even for the Japanese, it was donated to the Buddhist temple Ryuko in Tochigi as a Kateki figure. Thus the Humanist could now be found standing in a sanctuary of the Far East representing the divine image of the creator of the good ship "Kateki" and the patron saint of all seafaring men. Although this story is purely incidental it still has a symbolical significance: The spirit of Europe extended to far places. Erasmus was one of the noblest lights and guardians of western civilization. It was his nature to be a preserver. Thus, although he clearly recognized and even attacked the failings of the medieval church, he was bound to find himself in opposition to Luther. But even Erasmus could not hold back the turbulence of those times.

Erasmus of Rotterdam, carved figure on the stern of a Dutch caravel.

ra inter mortales diſi/
ſidia naſci. Mea κο/
λακία) .i. adulatio,
quam pediſſequã fe/
cit. ῥᾷον ἄγοντες) .i.
facile agentes. Sic &
Terentius, q̃uos fa/
cillime agitis, de diui
tibus loquens, quo/
rum uita facilior, &
expedita, Theocri/
tus itẽ in Cyclope, οὔ
τω γ οὖν ῥᾷῖζα δ'ἰαγ̄
ὁ κύκλωψ ὁ παρ' ἡμῖν
.i. Sic igitur facillime
egit Cyclops apud
nos. Ficulnus ille)
Alluſit ad Horatia/
nũ Priapũ, quẽ ille fi/
culnũ facit in ſatyris.
Olim truncꝰ erã ficul
nus inutile lignũ. Tũ
Græcis quicqd cõtẽ
nunt, ficulnum dici/
tur, ut in ſuis Chilia
adibꝰ teſtat̃ Eraſmꝰ.

mea κολακία primas tenet, cui cũ Momo
non magis cõuenit, q̃ cum agno lupis.
Itaq̃ ſublato illo iam multo licentius ac
ſuauius nugantur dij uere, ῥᾷον ἄγοντες, ut
inquit Homerus, nullo uidelicet cẽſore.
Quos enim non præbet iocos ficulnus
ille Priapus? Quos non ludos exhibet
furtis ac præſtigijs ſuis Mercuriꝰ? Quin
& Vulcanus ipſe in deorum cõuiuijs γε
λωτοποιῶν agere conſueuit, ac modo clau/
dicatione, modo cauillis, modo ridicu/
lis dictis exhilarare compotationẽ. Tũ
& Silenus ille ſenex amator, τὴν κόρδακα,
ſaltare ſolitus, una cum Polyphemo, τὴν
ξεταυλό, Nymphis τὴν γυμνοπόδιον ſaltan
tibꝰ. Satyri ſemicapri atellanas agitant.
Pan inſulſa quapiã cantiuncula riſum
audire mu/

Ac præſtigijs) Lucianus narrat illum Vulcani fccipẽ furatum. Itẽ Apol/
linis boues, tum & ſagittas præſtigijs ademit. γελωτοποιόν) .i. Morionem,
ſic enim uocant Græci, qui riſum mouere ſtudeat. Sic apud Homerum, Vul
canus in conuiuio deorum miniſtrat, & claudicatiõe riſum mouet. Tum ca
licem porrigens matri ridicula quædam loquitur, ut rixã diſcutiat inter Io/
uem & Iunonem. Vnde Homerus loquẽs de Vulcano Iliados. A. Ασβεςℴ
δ' ἄρα ζῶῶρρ γέλως μακάρεσσι θεοῖσιμ ὡς ἴδομ ἥφαιϛομ διὰ δ'ῶματα ποιπνύ
ονᴛα.i. Inextinguibilis igitur motus eſt riſus beatis dijs, Vt uiderẽt Vulca
num per domus ſeruientem. Senex amator) Hic nymphas perſequitur, &
inſidiatur apud Ouidium. τὴν κόρδακα) Cordax genus ridiculæ ſaltatio
nis ac ruſticanæ, cuius meminit Lucianus in libro de ſaltatiõe, meminit &
Pollux libro quarto, capite.xiij. περὶ εἰδῶν ὀρχήσεως. τὴν ξεταυλό.) Vox
ficta, qua repreſentaṫ ſaltatio Cyclopis Polyphemi, unde & Horatius, Salta
ret uti Cyclopa rogabat. Meminit Ariſtophanes in Pluto. γυμνοπόδιομ) &
hoc ſaltatiõis genꝰ a nuditate pedũ dictũ, γυμνὸμ eĩ nudũ, πούς pes dicit̃.
Attellanas) Attellanæ ſaltationis eſt genus in quo, obſcenis geſticulationi/
bus libido repreſentabaṫ, ab Atella ciuitate uocatũ. Pan.) Nam & is fiſtu
lam habet

76

Erasmus of Rotterdam, 1523, by Hans Holbein the Younger.

Left page: page illustrated by Hans Holbein the Younger in the
Praise of Folly, a work by Erasmus.

Afflictions of the Body

The scourge of medieval man lay in the plagues, the pox, St. Anthony's Fire, and innumerable other epidemic maladies which at this time could spread undeterred far and wide because of inferior medical skills and imperfect sanitary precautions. People lived in perpetual fear of death. About 1500 still another disease, syphilis, appeared with sudden and abrupt virulence. Painful surgical treatments—administered without anesthetics—such as amputations, cauteries, and other operations, together with the wretched conditions in the hospitals, all seemed to do nothing but aggravate the terror felt by all in the face of the infirmities of the body.

Allegorical picture showing Poverty, Sickness, Lust, and Death impeding man's ascent to heaven, from the 1531 edition of the book of Marcus Tullius Cicero, *Of the Virtuous Offices.*

ALTERIVS NON SIT QVI SVVS ESSE POTEST.

LAVS DEO, PAX VIVIS, REQVIES ÆTERNA SEPVLTVS.

OMNE DONVM PERFECTVM À DEO, IMPERE, À DIABO.

AVREOLVS PHILIPPVS THEOPHPRASTVS.

Paracelsus, a contemporary drawing.

Paracelsus

Among the men who endeavored to bring some measure of relief to mankind in this time of hopelessness was the physician Theophrastus Bombastus of Hohenheim, known as Paracelsus, an immediate contemporary of Luther (1493-1541). Though even his insights are clouded by the influence of astrology and alchemy, he contributed to the advance of medical science by recognizing that the causes of disease were scientifically identifiable and trying to overcome these ills with the chemical elements contained in his medicines.

79

Death and the merchant, from *The Dance of Death* by Hans Holbein the Younger.

Death and the physician, from *The Dance of Death* by Hans Holbein the Younger.

Mange, from *Depiction of Ailments* by Hans Weiditz.

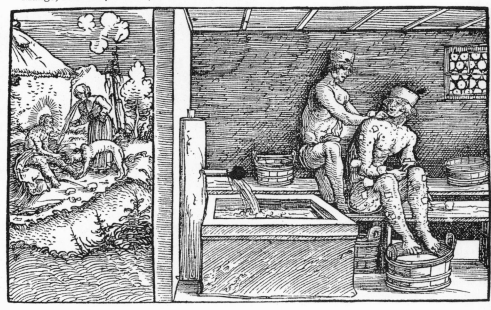

Death and the preacher, from *The Dance of Death* by Hans Holbein the Younger.

Death and the lovers, from *The Dance of Death* by Hans Holbein the Younger.

Dropsy, from *Depiction of Ailments* by Hans Weiditz.

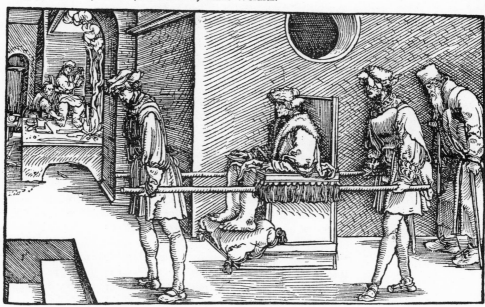

Sorcery and witchcraft, book illustration by Hans Schäufelin.

Witchcraft Witchcraft, too, was very much a part of the total picture of the church of the late Middle Ages. The witch hunts directed against the sorcerers and witches who were alleged to band together in congregations of Satan ultimately led to mass psychoses and legalistic excesses. The Witches' Hammer, a treatise by two Dominicans, H. Krämers (known as Institoris) and Jacob Sprenger, a professor of theology, reduced the entire madness to a system, which was then dealt with in a bull issued by Pope Innocent VIII.

Torture, Murder, and Death

Helplessly exposed to the forces of nature, the epidemics, and the vulgar commotion of the world around him, medieval man lived a harsh and burdensome life. He had a different attitude than we do today toward the brutal methods of torture, harsh judicial sentences, and the ways in which these sentences were executed. Even the respectable citizen was confronted every hour of the day with death in all its forms, and constantly had before his eyes the punishment of God manifested in the afflictions and the agonies of suffering. The arts did not hesitate to pictorialize these realities of daily life.

Torture, as depicted by a contemporary artist.

Executions, as depicted by a contemporary artist.

The Black Art

Of all the phenomena which at the turn of the century heralded a new era, the extension of the art of printing and its products was the one that most vividly portrayed the upheavals then underway. At the same time printing was the medium which intensified the unrest of the times and increased and hardened the conflicts between the contending forces. For the first time in the history of mankind a means of communication and an instrument to sway the masses appeared on the scene. Its potential effectiveness was unbounded and its influence was that which only the printed word and the reproduced picture can have. Approximately sixty years had elapsed between Gutenberg's first edition of the printed Bible and the printing of Luther's *Ninety-five Theses*, and by 1500, instead of just one printing press in Mainz, there were two hundred presses located in fifty different cities. Now the potential of Gutenberg's invention to influence the masses was set in motion. As editions increased in number, the prices of printed works decreased, thereby guaranteeing a wide circulation. During the Middle Ages an illuminated manuscript represented an enormous investment. For example, in 1074 Diemund von Wessobrunn purchased a country estate and paid for it with a two-volume illuminated manuscript that she herself had made. The skins of four hundred lambs and calves had gone into these volumes. In 1454 a copy of the Gutenberg Bible still cost forty-two gulden. At that time an ox represented a value of three gulden, so the cost of the Bible was equivalent to fourteen oxen. It is astonishing to note how many copies of the first printed Bible were published and how well they sold. The first edition numbered three thousand copies and was sold out within three months. A second edition of three thousand copies was exhausted within the year. Thus from a financial standpoint Gutenberg's invention opened up the possibility of unusual profits. Luther's New Testament in German—less voluminous than the Gutenberg Bible—was priced at only one and a half gulden, the equivalent of a maid's annual wage. In addition to books intended for more permanent usage there soon appeared the more short-term literature of the day: pamphlets, tracts, sermons, polemical challenges and their responses, and the circular, with its sensational daily bits of news.

The Type-foundryman, The Paper-maker,
the Printer, and the Bookbinder, by Jost Ammann
in *The Picture Series of the Trades*.

Vmb gelt ein sack vol ablas.

Regnum.

Diaboli.

Contemporary circular entitled *The seven-headed papal beast.*

Schawet an das siben hewbtig tier
Gantz eben der gstalt vnd manier
Wie Johannes geschen hat
Ein tier an des meres gstat
Das hat siben vngeleicher haubt
Eben wie diß pabstier gelaubt
Die waren all gekrönt bedewt
Die blatten der gaistlichen lewt
Das thier das het auch zehen horen
Deüt der gaistlig gwalt vn rumoren
Das thier trüg Gottes lesterung

Bedeüt jr verfürische zung
Das thier was aim pardel geleich
Bedeüt des Bapst mordische reich
Das auch hinricht durch tiranney
Alles was jm entgegen sey
Auch so hat das thier peren füß
Deüt das das Euangeli süß
Ist von dem bastum vndertretten
Verschart/verdecket vn zerknetten
Das thier het auch ains löwen mund
Bedeüt deß bapstum weiten schlund

Den doch gar nie erfüllen thetten
Aples/pallium noch annatten
Bann/opfer/peicht/stifft zü Gotsdienst
Land vnd leüt Künigreich rent vn zinst
Das es alles hat in sich verschlunden
Das thier entpfieng ain tödlich wunden
Deüt das Doctor Martin hat gschriben
Das bapstum tödlich wund gebliben
Mit dem otten des Herren mund
Gott geb das es gar gee zü grund
Amen.

Ein grausam Meerwunder/den Bapst

bedeutende/zu Rom gefunden/vnd zu Wittemberg erstlich Anno 23. vñ darnach abermal Anno 46.mit der auslegung Philippi gedruckt.

Mit einer Vorrede Matthiæ Flacij Illyrici.

Circular directed against the papacy by Christian Rödinger, a printer, 1546.

Ulrich von Hutten, woodcut from his *Booklet of Conversations* of the year 1521.

Ulrich von Hutten

Ulrich von Hutten came from a family of knights. He grew up in the tradition of feuds and wars, the normal milieu of knighthood. Later, however, he was marked out for the priesthood and his life took a different course. He became a scholar whose political instinct attracted him to the common people. When Luther, whose enthusiastic follower he became, appeared on the scene, he saw how through Luther's writings a mass movement was born among the people. He noted how effective the German language could be and began to write in German. He was able to arouse and enthuse the spirits of the people. Gutenberg had already created the technical means for influencing the masses, and Luther had supplied the requisite language. Hutten was the first to combine the two into a political instrument. He combined the attitude of the knight and his militant spirit with the weapons of the pen and the word and became Germany's first political writer. However, his end is marked by resignation, sickness, and banishment.

Milestones Along the Way

A Beginning and a Departure

On November 11, 1483, the day after his birth, Martin Luther was baptized in the church at Eisleben. A year after Martin's birth his father moved to Mansfeld where the young lad attended the local Latin School and where he learned those things which the school of his day had to offer: monastic Latin, writing, singing, and a little arithmetic. Although Luther, like many other people of prominence, retained no excessively fond memories of his schooldays, he probably owed more to the school than he admitted. It provided him with a solid academic foundation. In 1497 he transferred to the school of the Brethren of the Common Life at Magdeburg. This brotherhood, with characteristics typical of a religious order, was probably the most attractive community of the Middle Ages and was a stronghold of genuine lay piety. It was inevitable that the fourteen-year-old boy would receive only the best impressions there. All further details are lacking. A prince from Anhalt, who as a mendicant subjected himself to the maximum effort in asceticism, impressed him, and of him he said, "Anyone who looked at him, had to smack his lips with prayerful devotion." Yet this was probably no more than a minor religious experience.

The direction which his inner development took became clearer when in the following year he arrived at Eisenach. All his life he continued to call it "his good city," and the happiest memories of his youth were associated with this period of his life. While here, he, like many of his schoolmates, sang in the streets for his daily subsistence, and was "discovered" by Mrs. Ursula Cotta, a noble, motherly woman. Her house was one of the most refined and devout homes in Eisenach. Luther's association with the large circle of splendid people whom he met there left such a mark on him for the rest of his life that his grateful estimate about his stay in Eisenach can be attributed largely to this impression.

The university was next. Perhaps it was only external reasons that prompted the father to choose the university of Erfurt rather than Leipzig, which was closer. Erfurt enjoyed the better scholastic reputation.

Beginning in 1501, Luther's first university years followed the normal and established framework of those days. The routine of his personal life was just as carefully regulated as his academic curriculum. In all these matters nothing unusual can be reported about him. He himself admitted that the routine disputations in which he had to engage helped greatly to develop his acute dialectic abilities. Even as a student he distinguished himself so much in them that he was nicknamed "the philosopher."

It is of no real significance that at that time he did not become a member of the Erfurt group of Humanists—this circle did not become active until Luther was already in the monastery. What is significant, however, is that he became acquainted with the "modern" theology of William of Occam. He accepted Occam's doctrine of the inability of human reason to comprehend the truths of revelation through its own resources, and later on gave new and forceful expression to this doctrine. Above all the more liberal attitude of the Occamists acquainted him with the current "modern" view of the universe and in this way he ultimately acquired a very sound and thoroughly independent knowledge of Aristotelian philosophy.

On July 2, 1505, he was returning from an unscheduled holiday, which for unknown reasons he had taken in the middle of the semester. While at Stotternheim, a few hours distant from Erfurt, a severe thunderstorm came up. A bolt of lightning struck the ground so close to him that the blast of air hurled him a distance of several yards. In his terror he cried out, "Help me, Saint Anne, I will become a monk!"

No matter how one may care to explain this in detail, the vow made to St. Anne, the patron saint of the miners, was the culmination of a long inner struggle. During the hours of leisure after his Master's examination and before commencing his further studies, this struggle had manifested itself in a manner peculiar to Luther. As he himself reported, he had suffered greatly under the temptation to be melancholy. It was based on anguish because of his sins.

It was this earnest conscientiousness which made him keep his vow despite all advice to the contrary. By July 16 he had arranged his affairs to the point that he could now invite his circle of friends to a final get-together. Early the following morning his companions accompanied him to the gate of the Black Monastery of the Augustinian Eremites. He was serious about his decision; more than this we do not know. This earnestness was now to lead him into some of the most grueling inner struggles of his life.

Interlude: The Journey to Rome

Luther's journey to Rome from the fall of 1510 until the spring of 1511 was a curious interlude. It was occasioned by a directive from Egidio Canisio of Viterbo, the General of his order. Canisio wanted to persuade those communities of the Augustinian order which were lax about observing the order's rule to accept the long-sought reforms and to unite them with other communities which had adopted the reforms. John Staupitz, who had become the provincial of the order in Saxony, had accepted this assignment, but at first he did not dare to carry it out. When the time finally came for bringing about this union, he met with resistance from the most austere, self-reformed chapters, and especially the two most influential monasteries of this province: Nürnberg and Erfurt. The congregation at Erfurt delegated the scholarly Father Nathin, and, as prescribed by the rules of the order, a travel companion, Father Luther. Thus it was that Luther got to Rome.

It is important to note the result this adventure had on his life. The idea that the first dramatic collision between two worlds took place here is completely wrong. It is true that Luther later on related how, at the famous site along the Via Cassia where one catches the first glimpse of the eternal city, he had fallen to his knees and cried, "Hail to thee, O Holy Rome!" But it is clear that the memories which an older Luther casually uttered in a conversation about his journey to Rome must be scrutinized with critical objectivity. Viewing all the facts in retrospect it seems to be an established fact that his pilgrimage to Rome did not bring about a significant change in his personality nor in his development as a reformer.

At first he was fully occupied with his business at the office of the Curia. During those months the headquarters of the Roman church was poorly staffed. The pope was away at some battlefront. Only two of the cardinals happened to be in Rome, and one of them was critically ill. The two German monks probably did not even have a conference with the curial secretary who handled such matters as those which brought them to Rome.

Luther, therefore, had time available in the holy city to see things for himself. The things that he was able to report later on were rather startling. In those days Rome gave the impression of being almost a rural city. Undoubtedly there was much more of interest to be found in Erfurt, Nürnberg, or Augsburg than in Rome. St. Peter's, the new great central church of

Christendom was still in its very early stages. In fact, Luther did not even mention this church. The impressions that he received and reported marked him as a medieval monk who, following the customs of his peers, availed himself of all the salvatory possibilities of this eternal city, who loyally and in good faith visited all the renowned worship centers—particularly those that offered indulgences—and who was interested in the methods of preaching and the worship practices of the Roman clergy. But he did all this with a most negative result. He also demonstrated an amazing lack of interest in the flowering art of the Renaissance. We are unable to point to a single remark by him that would indicate a genuine relationship between him and this new art. In Florence, then in its artistic prime, he was interested in the fate of Savonarola, but even more in the charitable activities of noblemen who personally devoted themselves to the care of the sick and the poor. But not a word did he say about Michelangelo's David! In defense of Luther it must be added that the newly blossoming art of the Renaissance had not yet significantly altered the outer appearance of Rome. At that time the great works of art were to be seen primarily in the houses and the courtyards. Luther observed the usual routine of the pious without seeing or hearing anything unusual and without attracting anyone's special attention. For his tours of the city he made use of the current pilgrim's guidebook, the *Mirabilia urbis Romae*. We shall have to believe his later assurances that he resorted to this guidebook not in order to expose himself to the magnetism of Rome's sights and scenes, but to be sure that he did not fail to visit any of those holy sites at which he, with all the fervor of his inwardly restless life, might seek forgiveness and indulgences. Later on he repeatedly denied that he had found these. Presumably the condition of his soul as he visited these holy places was typically that of a medieval man who was still firmly encased in the religious convictions of those days.

Thus we are not surprised that he failed to record his impressions as we might expect. The fact that he returned without any basic impression of the pope or of the Curia is due to the circumstances noted above, namely, that the papal court was then not even in Rome. He did not see a single leading personality of the Catholic church of that day. Even the impression made by the sanctuaries which he visited conscientiously—the seven main churches which a pilgrim had to visit in good conscience and in a state of total fasting before he was admitted to the eucharist at St. Paul's—suffered under the pressure of this spiritual busyness. In all this the conscientious German struck the Italians as being ponderous and awkward, while the

Italian priests could "celebrate their mass with such assurance and elegance, now this way, now that, as though they were jugglers." Next to the undisguised faithlessness of these priests he was offended most by the tempo with which they discharged their duty at mass, as well as the impatience with which they expressed themselves to the stranger in the repeated call to him: "*passa, passa*—hurry, hurry!"

Later on, his recollections of this trip dealt mainly with those things which might be expected of a son of peasant stock who had learned to appraise people and places according to their practical worth. He wasted no words on the hardships his journey must have entailed. The rules of the order demanded that the two friars travel on foot. From all the reports that we possess today, it is certain that the weather at that time was unpleasant and bad. In Rome rain fell incessantly in torrents until the middle of February. In addition there was the hike across the wintry Alps and back again. Even in later years the traveler never mentioned a single word about the feat of physical endurance performed by him and his companion.

The psychologist, however, cannot refrain from adding that Luther was still completely immersed in that stage of life that must be described as creative solitude.

> Who truth must speak and soon proclaim
> Now broods in silence deep within;
> Who later lightning must enflame
> Must long a darkling cloud have been.

Luther was still in that stage of life during which impressions are gathered, heaped up, and stored away for life's future explosive accomplishments. It happens not infrequently that creative genius requires a longer period of intellectual preparation and provisioning than the nimble careerist.

But a more profound meaning must be discerned in this curious aloofness of Luther toward the Rome of the early High Renaissance. It is simply not possible to regard him primarily or even exclusively as a product of the Renaissance. If we had not already deduced it from his great disputes with Erasmus, then certainly his behavior would have made it abundantly clear that he was not attaching himself to the stream of an intellectual and historical development, but that a certain something else that was weightier than an intellectual renewal had been thrust upon him.

Pope Julius II
being borne on
his throne,
drawing by
Raphael.

Martin Luther in 1520, copper engraving by Lucas Cranach the Elder.

The Pope and the Monk

The entrance of the pope into St. Peter's Basilica on the portable
throne of Byzantine emperors, surrounded by noblemen of the papal
court and Swiss guards, is reminiscent of the splendor, the triumph,
and very presence of a secular sovereign who is flanked by his
marching soldiers. In contrast to this sketch by Raphael is the earliest
portrayal of Luther, the masterful engraving from the year 1520,
called Luther as a monk, *by Lucas Cranach the Elder. Cranach's*
humble inscription states that "Luther himself graved the image
of his spirit, Cranach's burin carved merely his mortal countenance."
In both a literal and figurative sense this engraving became the new
ideal symbolizing that day.

95

Luther's Parents: The Great "Mountain Cry"

P. 205

Writing about his ancestral origins Luther himself stated: "I come from a family of peasants. My great-grandfather, my grandfather, and my father actually tilled the soil. As Philip Melanchthon once said, by rights I should have become a magistrate or mayor or some other kind of village official, some kind of foreman in charge of others. After that, my father moved to Mansfeld and there became a miner. . . . My mother had to carry all the wood home on her back. That was how they reared us. They had to endure the kind of great hardship that the world would not tolerate today."

This description by Luther, however, shifts the real problems of his ancestry and education. It is true that the heritage of his peasant ancestry was decisive for his personality. But his father—as Luther himself writes—was only a poor miner in his youth. He quickly worked his way up during those years of upheaval within the mining industry in Mansfeld and Saxony, during the great "Mountain Cry," as those years of economic boom and social restructuring in the mining industry were called. He became an entrepreneur and attained a moderate level of prosperity. Because of this he had high hopes for his son's future. Until the years of his manhood Luther suffered greatly from feelings of guilt because of the disappointment which he caused his father by entering the monastery, in other words, by crushing his father's hopes that Martin might achieve prominence in the coterie of

the better lawyers. After all, the father had raised the funds to finance his son's studies at the university with difficulty.

All his life Luther found it difficult to overcome a child's fear of parental strictness. "One should not whip children too severely. One day father thrashed me so harshly that I fled from him and he became afraid until he had once again won me over to him."

"My parents kept me under the most rigid control, in fact, to the point of intimidation. Because of one nut, mother once beat me until blood flowed. This harsh discipline finally drove me into the monastery. Although they meant well, I was, in the long run, merely intimidated. They were unable to maintain a proper balance between a person's natural inclination and the subsequent punishment. One ought to punish in such a way that the apple lies next to the rod."

Although the later reconciliation with his father led to a more mellow judgment, his conversations, even in his advanced age, still contained echoes of the terrors of his youth, of the fear of parental harshness, of the dread of the schoolmasters' cruel punishments. In the course of his *Table Talk* in the years 1537 and 1543 Luther said, "It is a bad thing when the faith of children and pupils in their parents and teachers is shaken. For example, there have been insensitive schoolmasters who ruined many excellent qualities by their callous ways."—"Many teachers are as cruel as the hangman. Thus one day just before noon I was paddled fifteen times, although I was not at fault, for I was supposed to decline and conjugate although I as yet had not learned how to do it."

Eisleben, engraving by Matthew Merian from Zeiller's *Topographia superioris Saxoniae.*

ANNO·1530·AM·29·TAG·IVNY·IST·HANS·LVTER
D·MARTINVS· VATER·INN·GOTT
VERSCHIE DENN

Hans Luther,
Martin's father,
painting by
Lucas Cranach
the Elder, now in
the Wartburg.

ANNO · 1531 · AM · 30 · TAG · IVNY · IST · MARG
ARETA LVTERIND · MA   RTIIVS · MVTTER
· INN · GOTT ·   · VERSCHIEDEN

Margaret,
Luther's mother,
painting by
Lucas Cranach
the Elder, now in
the Wartburg.

Mansfeld, engraving by Matthew Merian in the *Topographia superioris Saxoniae*.

A schoolmaster's show-card, detail from a painting by Ambrosius Holbein.

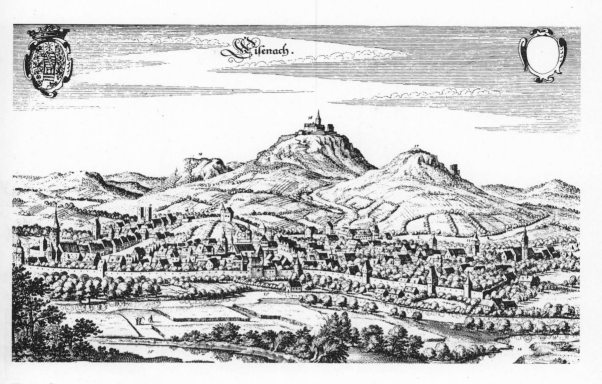

Eisenach, engraving by Matthew Merian from the *Topographia superioris Saxoniae.*

School Days

When Luther embarked upon his later career he was not unprepared. From the very beginning his father had been intent on furthering his boy's natural abilities. Having completed the course at the parish school at Mansfeld from 1488 to 1496, Luther, at the age of fourteen, went to Magdeburg to attend the school of the Brethren of the Common Life. Probably because of the large numbers of relatives living there, he then transferred in 1497 to Eisenach, where he attended St. George's Parish School until 1501.

101

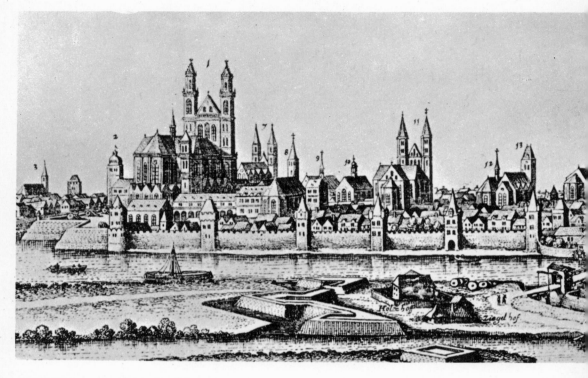

Magdeburg, engraving by Matthew
Merian from the *Topographia superioris
Saxoniae.*

Monastery school,
a contemporary woodcut.

Magdeburg

From the days of his stay at Magdeburg in the school of the Brethren of the Common Life, a religious community that emphasized biblical piety rather than theological speculation, Luther recalled an experience which must have had some minor effect on him: "In those days I saw with my own eyes a Duke of Anhalt . . . walking along the wide street, wearing the hood of the barefooted Augustinians and like a mule carrying a sack on his back that was so heavy that he was bent to the ground. His fellow monks walked unhampered alongside him so that the devout duke might, by himself, serve as an example of sanctity to all the world. They had gotten him to the point where he engaged in all the menial tasks in the monastery just like the other friars. He had fasted, kept vigils, and so flagellated himself that he looked like death itself, all skin and bones. In fact, he died soon after that. . . . Anyone who looked at him had to smack his lips with prayerful devotion and be ashamed of his own worldliness."

Luther at Erfurt Today's visitor to Erfurt can still sense something of the importance of that city during the Middle Ages as a Hanseatic town, a center of commerce, an intellectual metropolis, especially when he has a view of the magnificent community-planned arrangement of the cathedral and the Church of St. Severus together with the magnificent, winding, terraced staircase rising upward between them.

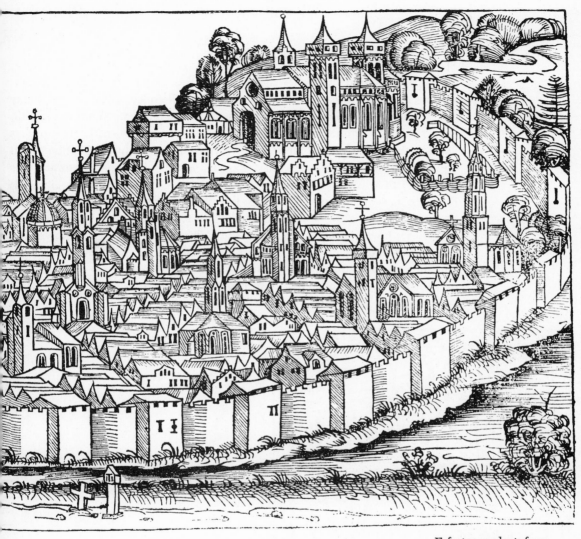

Erfurt, woodcut from Schedel's history of the world from the year 1493.

Here one can sense something of the spirit that once inspired the entire city. The first European university with the four basic faculties existed here at Erfurt. At about the time of Luther's birth, it opened its doors to Humanism and enjoyed halcyon days. Eighteen years later, in 1501, Luther matriculated as a student and began his studies in the faculty of fine arts.

At the University

Speaking of life at the University of Erfurt, Luther narrated very vividly: "In times past that university had such a large student body that by comparison other universities were regarded as small colleges. Of course, today this splendor has completely disappeared and vanished. What a magnificent sight the conferring of the Master's degrees was—with the torches leading the procession! I don't believe that any worldly celebration could equal it. The greatest pageantry was displayed when the doctorate was conferred; it was the custom to ride on horseback all around the city. All that has now fallen into discard. I wish it were still observed today." Speaking of those days he also said: "Thirty years ago no one read the Bible and it was unknown to all people. The prophets were unknown and not understandable. When I was twenty years old, for example, I still had never seen a Bible. I was under the impression that no other Gospel or Epistle existed except for those recorded in the Sunday postils. Finally

University lecture, a contemporary woodcut.

Conferring the Master's degree, woodcut by Hans Weiditz.

I found a Bible in the university library and read a passage in the book of kings (I Sam. 1) dealing with the mother of Samuel. The book appealed to me in a wonderful way and I knew that I would consider myself fortunate if I could some day own such a book. . . . But then the sound of the bell summoned me to my class lecture."

Even though he was a young student, the serious mood of the times burdened his life. For a while the plague raged in the city and, we are told, claimed one of his close friends. Then he himself was brought to the brink of death by a minor accident. In the neighborhood of Erfurt, during a journey on foot back to his home, he accidentally jabbed his sword into his thigh and cut the main artery. A surgeon was summoned from the city and barely managed to save his life, for Luther was on the verge of bleeding to death. In Luther's narrative of this accident one can sense that fear of death which some time later inspired in him the vow to become a monk.

The Monk

Luther had now studied for four years and completed the basic studies
required in the liberal arts by earning the Master of Arts degree. In 1505
at the Faculty of Law he began the studies based on the courses he had
just completed. At that time an inner upheaval, not understood even by
those who were close to him, impelled him on July 16, 1505, to enter
the Erfurt monastery of the Augustinian Eremites, one of the mendicant
orders. Luther himself recounted this event in a *Table Talk* of July 16,
1539, in the following manner: "On the Feast of St. Alexius he [Luther]
said: 'This is the anniversary of the day when I entered the monastery
at Erfurt.' Then he began to relate the story of how he had made a vow,

when hardly fourteen days before on the road near Stotternheim not far from Erfurt he had been so violently shaken by a bolt of lightning that in his fright he called out, 'Help me, Saint Anne, I will become a monk!'—But God interpreted my vow according to the Hebrew translation: Anna means 'by grace,' and therefore not according to 'the law.'—Later on I regretted this vow, and many advised me to disregard it. But I remained firm and on the day before Alexius I invited my best friends for a farewell dinner and asked them to accompany me on the following day to the monastery. When they held back, I told them, 'Today you see me for the last time!' Tearfully, they then escorted me. . . . My father was very angry about this vow, but I persisted in my decision. I never intended to leave the monastery. I had died completely to the world."

In September Luther made a general confession of sins, whereupon he was accepted on a probationary basis as a novice within the monastic community. He received the tonsure and the habit of the order. He pledged to dedicate himself as a sacrifice to God and the order, and to live the rest of his life without possessions and in chastity, according to the rules of St. Augustine. In the course of the following months he received the threefold ordination, followed on May 2, 1507, by the celebration of his first mass.

The oldest exterior view of the Augustinian Monastery at Erfurt.

The Great Doubt

Luther did not find in monasticism the peace which he had sought.
In later life he again and again described the terrors and agonies which
then unduly oppressed and tormented him. "It is true that I was a
devout monk and observed the rules of my order so rigidly that
I can say: If any monk ever got to heaven through monkery, then I
too should have made it. All my monastery companions who knew
me will testify to that. In fact, if it had lasted much longer, I should
have killed myself with vigils, praying, reading, and other labors. . . .
For when even a minor temptation approached me from the realm
of death or sin, I broke down and found that neither baptism nor
monkery helped me. In this way I had long ago lost Christ and
his baptism. I was the most miserable monk in this world, my days
and nights were so heavy with such lament and despair that no one
could help me."

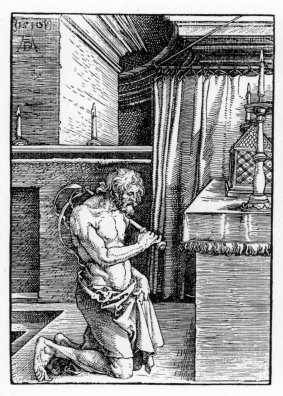

Tombstone of John Zacharias (1428), bitter foe of John Huss, at the main altar of the Augustinian church at Erfurt, and the very site at which Luther, during the rite of ordination to the priesthood, prostrated himself.

On the left page:
A flagellant, woodcut by Albrecht Dürer.

The sacrifice of the mass, a contemporary woodcut.

New Studies— New Tasks

A monk, woodcut serving as a book illustration.

The young priest's superiors soon noticed his intellectual gifts. They undoubtedly also recognized his problematical spiritual disposition and endeavored to guide the self-accusations of this penitent monk wrestling for the salvation of his soul into more fruitful channels. The person of John von Staupitz now gradually came to the fore. Born in 1460, he had served as adviser to Elector Frederick the Wise in laying plans for the founding of the University of Wittenberg in 1502. He became Vicar General of the Augustinians in Germany in 1503, at the same time occupying a chair of theology at Wittenberg. During his monastic years Luther enjoyed an almost filial relationship to Staupitz, who not only aided him pastorally but, as his superior and paternal friend, repeatedly intervened to direct the course of his life. But we must not fail to realize that like Luther's natural father, this man, too, in the last

Paradise and hell, a contemporary woodcut.

A monk with a quill and penknife, woodcut used as a book illustration.

analysis, was not able to cope with Luther's temperament and was ultimately overwhelmed by the movement which Luther later on set in motion with his ninety-five Theses. In the spirit of resignation he stepped down from the stage of history, into whose limelight Luther had from time to time propelled him. But all this still lay fifteen years in the future. Soon after his first mass, Luther was commissioned to study theology. Within a year Staupitz summoned him to Wittenberg where he entrusted him with a professorial chair of moral philosophy. Concurrently he earned the Bachelor of Theology degree in 1509. Thereupon he was once again recalled to Erfurt. For the next three years he taught dogmatics within the general studies program. In 1512 Staupitz resigned from his teaching post at Wittenberg and entrusted Luther with his own professorial chair. Luther was now twenty-nine years of age.

113

LUTHER ABOUT STAUPITZ

If Staupitz or rather God through Staupitz had not helped me out of my afflictions, I would have drowned in them and long ago been in hell.

All things that are mine I have received through Staupitz, who helped me to find them.

JANUARY TO MARCH, 1532

Then I heeded your word as though it had been a word from heaven: namely, that there can be no true repentance unless it begins with the love of righteousness and of God; and that the beginning of repentance is to be found at the very point that the others consider to be its goal and culmination.

This word of yours was imbedded in me like "the sharp arrows of a strong man," and I began at once to compare it with the Scriptural passages that deal with repentance.

LETTER TO STAUPITZ, MAY 30, 1518

Even though I may no longer be acceptable to you nor in your good favor, it is not proper for me to forget you with ingratitude, for it was through you that the light of the Gospel for the first time shined forth in our heart out of the darkness.

LETTER TO STAUPITZ, SEPTEMBER 17, 1523

Unless he [Luther] wants to be an accursed, ungrateful mule, he must boast that Staupitz was first of all the father of his teachings and brought him to birth in Christ.

LETTER TO THE ELECTOR OF SAXONY, 1545

Legend on the bottom of the Salzburg picture of Staupitz:
John IV, abbot of St. Peter's at Salzburg, born in Thuringia of the noble family of von Staupitz, at first a monk in the Order of the Augustinian Eremites, Doctor of Sacred Theology, and Martin Luther's father confessor, prior, and provincial; thereafter councillor and cathedral preacher of His Eminence Cardinal Matthias Lang, Archbishop of Salzburg, finally consecrated by papal dispensation to the Order of St. Benedict in the Monastery of St. Peter on August 1, 1522, and on the following day legally and unanimously elected and elevated to the abbotship, where, after having assiduously administered the affairs of his office. for two years and five months, his destiny was fulfilled on December 20, 1525. He was buried in the Chapel of St. Vitus.

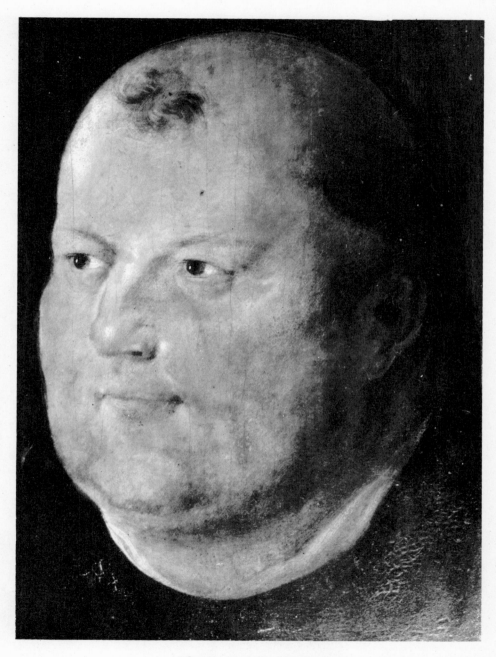

John von Staupitz, painting by an unknown master, now in
the Gallery of the Archabbey of St. Peter's at Salzburg.

Rome

Before Luther finally settled in Wittenberg he was commissioned by his order to travel to Rome in connection with the internal affairs of his order. His journey lasted from the middle of November, 1510, to the beginning of April, 1511. In later years he recalled his emotions as he approached the center of Christendom: "When I first saw Rome, I fell to the ground, lifted my hands, and said, 'Hail to thee, O Holy Rome!' Yes, it is a truly holy place because of the sainted martyrs and the blood which they shed there."

Rome, a painting now in the Vatican Library, showing the Piazza del Populo with S. Maria del Populo and the monastery in which Luther lodged during his sojourn in the city.

Old St. Peter's Church and the Medieval Plaza

The journey on foot from central Germany to Rome required about seven weeks. While in the city Luther had enough time to become acquainted with its sights and to devote himself to his own personal edification. There were a number of travel guides for tourists in Rome and we are able to get an idea of what Luther had an opportunity to see. The picture by Maarten van Heemskerk shows the exact condition of St. Peter's Plaza and the facade of the old St. Peter's Church prior to its demolition. Countless devout pilgrims had wandered across this plaza before Luther. Bearing the marks of the centuries, it seemed like a many-tiered stage setting. The triple-floored Loggia next to the entrance to St. Peter's was begun during the reign of Paul II (1464-1471), and for 150 years was the place from which the popes pronounced the solemn benediction urbi et orbi ("to city and world").

St. Peter's Plaza with the Vatican and the old St. Peter's Church, drawing by Maarten van Heemskerk.

Pilate's Staircase

In one of his last sermons (November 15, 1545) Luther spoke of his experience on Pilate's staircase in Rome. According to tradition it was once part of Pilate's palace in Jerusalem and was revered as the site where Pilate confronted and condemned Jesus. By climbing the Scala Sancta on one's knees it was possible to release a soul from purgatory. The text from the 1491 Roman guidebook quoted on this page adds further details. In his sermon Luther had this to say: "As a monk I did everything and still I did not know whether this found favor with God. This is the way I had been taught under the papacy. Likewise, when I had read the seven canonical hours, I had to say that I did not know whether this was acceptable to God. Of what value was that prayer? When in Rome I wanted to release one of my ancestors from purgatory. I went up Pilate's staircase, praying a Pater Noster on every step. It was generally believed that if a person prayed like this he would redeem a soul. But when I got to the top I thought to myself: 'Who knows whether it is true?'"

Item do ist ein steinen stieg da bey hat.ix. vnd acht staffel die was zu Hierusalem an Pylatus hauß auff der selben stiege wartt christus vor pylatū gefuret vnd verurteilet vnnd wer die stiege in andacht vff oder aß geet der hat als offt er das tūt von yeð staf fel.ix.iar ablas.vnd an der selben staffel do ist ein eisenes gegitter ist ob einem crūtzlein da ist die genade zweyfaltig. an der selben stat ist cristus vff die knie gefallen. wer die stiege knien auff get.der erlost damit ein se le fur die er pit.solt die sele pyß an den iung sten tag im fegfeur sein.so offtei n staffel so offt ein pater noster vnd ein aue maria ge sprochen.vñ hēr nyden bey der stiege ist ein eren haubt vnd ein hant mit einer kūgel ge standen.sten nu im Capitolio.die kūgel be deut die welt die hant die romer vntter irē gewalt gehabt.oßen gen der stiegen stet ein weiße steinen seul.die ist in der mit erspaltē geleich do cristus gecreutzigt wart.

Two pages from the 1491 German edition of *Mirabilia urbis Romae*. Above, a woodcut showing the altar of St. Veronica.
Below, the page dealing with Pilate's staircase.

Luther as a monk, on a coin by an unknown woodcarver probably from Upper Germany.

A HARSH JUDGMENT

"I would not trade my visit to Rome for a hundred thousand gulden. If I had not seen it with my own eyes, I would not believe it. Godlessness and evil are so rampant and bold there that no attention is paid to either God or man, to sin or shame. All the devout people who have been there will testify to this, as well as all the godless ones who returned from Italy as worse people than when they went there. My main reason for traveling to Rome was to make a general confession that started with the sins of my youth and then to become a pious person, even though I had made such a confession twice before in Erfurt. But in Rome I came across the most ignorant people. O dear Lord God, how can the cardinals know anything, burdened as they are with a mass of administrative trivia! Things are complicated enough for those of us who devote ourselves to our studies hour after hour and day after day."

Wittenberg in Luther's day, a contemporary copper engraving.

The Doctor of Theology

After brief sojourns in Augsburg and Nürnberg Luther returned to Erfurt in April of 1511. His position within his order now began to be strengthened, and Staupitz paved his way toward a meaningful career, for which the degree of Doctor of Theology was to serve as a foundation, since Staupitz intended to recommend Luther to the Elector as his successor. For this reason he was transferred to Wittenberg after a convention of his order at Cologne had elected him subprior of the monastery at Wittenberg.

All his life Luther looked upon his doctorate as more than an academic degree. For him it was the cornerstone of all his biblical-theological labors and the definitive commission for his work as a reformer. In one of his *Table Talks* between December 14 and 26, 1531, he described the events that led to the earning of the Doctor's degree: "Staupitz, my prior, once sat pensively under the pear tree which still stands in the center of my yard.

Finally he said to me, 'Master Martin, you should earn your doctorate, for you will have some real work to do.'—Four years after I had received the doctorate this came true.—When he again approached me under the pear tree in the same manner, I cited a number of arguments in my defense, stressing above all that my energies had been so drained that I could not hope for a long life. Staupitz answered, 'Don't you know that our Lord God has many great things to do? Therefore he needs many intelligent and wise people who will help by advising him. Regardless when you die, you must still be his counselor.'

"But in those days I never realized that this prophecy would be fulfilled in the manner in which it actually was: four years later I began my struggle against the pope and the entire papacy."

The years between 1512 and 1517 were the years of Luther's inner conversion. The act of posting the Theses was the outcome—as were all decisive acts in Luther's life—of a long period of preparation and clarification of his thinking. It was centered in the spiritual afflictions which exhausted him physically. By referring to his lectures and personal testimonies we are able to trace Luther's development with a great degree of accuracy. The great landmark of this development was the so-called tower experience, a spiritual illumination that took place in the tower room of the Black Monastery at Wittenberg. It probably occurred at the beginning of 1513 while he was preparing his lectures on the Psalms scheduled to start in August of that year.

Receipt written in Luther's own hand acknowledging the fifty gulden which the Elector had sent him as payment of the fee for his doctoral examination.

The Birth of the Reformation

Inner Turmoil

In 1511 Luther came to Wittenberg for the second time. High hopes were held for gifted young Brother Martin by his order, and above all by the vicar-general, John von Staupitz.

During the winter of 1508 Luther had at first lectured only in a provisional capacity at the University of Wittenberg, and it was not until 1511 that he fully assumed the professorship vacated by Staupitz. It seems that Luther's departure from Erfurt in 1511 was not without some unpleasant disagreement with several brothers of the order and possibly even with some of his superiors. Apparently there were some who were envious of the man who was already rising to prominence. At that time no one could foresee that Luther would never again leave Wittenberg and that he would make this unimpressive little town of no more than two thousand inhabitants, which according to him was located "on the frontier of civilization," the scene of momentous historical decisions.

Least of all did Luther himself foresee what lay ahead. For a long time his spirits had been torn by severe inner conflicts. We know of the tremendous earnestness with which during his monastery days he observed the religious practices recommended by the church of the Middle Ages to those concerned about the salvation of their souls. Still regarding monasticism completely as a refuge for the soul which could guarantee him eternal salvation, Luther engaged in all these practices with exemplary devotion. None of the countless religious practices, none of the many opportunities for self-examination and for the attainment of the church's absolution could meet his needs, because he was involved in one of those decisions in which the external quantity of effort expended was of almost negligible significance. The thing at stake here was a new way of life. His heart found no peace even after he had confessed his sins with the radical seriousness of a person ready to dismember his very soul. More than once, just a few minutes after he had been to confession, he would try to buttonhole a passing priest from the order in order to make another confession. All the means of grace offered to him by the piety of the monastic life—the Bible, the breviary, theological and other labors—he imbued with the same driving seriousness and pointed them toward the one invisible center of the struggle then going on within him. He was a person who simply had to pass through all the fires of hell.

It is true that he was a spiritual fighter. But he was also a sufferer who—although today it is difficult to cull this from the intellectual forms which his struggle assumed—anticipated and vicariously won the victory in the struggle toward a full faith for succeeding centuries. He suffered that which but few mentors of Christendom after him were able to describe on the basis of their own personal experience, namely, trials and temptations. Of what did these consist?

Certainly not in any obvious "need," as, for example, in some sexual problem. We know that in this respect Luther was not subjected to any particular conflicts. Nor did his trials consist of intellectual doubts that might have resulted from the ideological irreconcilability between the new view of the universe and the biblical concept of the world. All this is a modern interpretation and does not in the least touch upon the real depth of Luther's inner need. The challenge to his soul was on a much more profound level. It took possession of his entire being and existence. It was the question whether it was possible for him to justify himself in God's sight. He was convinced that unless he found an answer to this problem, he was lost. Therein lay the core of his inner struggle: on the one hand faith was solely the deed and gift of God's action descending from outside of man and toward him, on the other hand he also looked upon faith as a direct, personal experience. As Wilhelm Pauck put it, "Escape from these antinomies into the Catholic order of things or into the inner light of the enthusiasts was impossible."

For Luther this question was sheathed in the mystery of "the righteousness of God." In the deep night into which his doubts had hurled him, there was an occasional assuring flash of light. Staupitz had helped with some words of consolation which Luther never forgot. He had first told Luther that trials were a normal part of any true Christian life. He had also tried to divert him from his religious scrupulosity, the worst foe of genuine penitential earnestness, by teaching him the difference between real and imagined sins. Above all Staupitz had tried to direct the struggling Luther toward the person of Christ as the source of comfort. There was profound theological and pastoral wisdom in the consoling word he spoke to the anxious young friar: "God is not angry with you—you are angry with God!"

But even Staupitz could not offer him the ultimate release from his spiritual struggles. There can hardly be any doubt that despite all his kindness and wisdom, the cultured but also reserved and dispassionate nature of Staupitz did not fully understand the radicalism of Luther's struggle. The road was his to walk alone. His scholarly activities, which had sometimes proved to be a comfort and a diversion, now plunged him into ever new abysses. He knew that unless he could find a solution to his struggles he would not only not be able to work and teach as a scholar, but he simply would no longer be able to live.

The Tower Experience

The day which finally brought him his answer has been described by Luther himself. Even today it is touching to read how a year before his death, in the preface to the first volume of the *Complete Edition of Luther's Latin Writings,* the aging Reformer speaks about that hour. The light of a supernal joy glows through these lines and they merit being added to the great confessional writings of church history in which outstanding Christians have recorded the hour of their confrontation with God. Luther writes: "Though I lived as a monk without reproach, I felt that I was a sinner before God with an extremely disturbed conscience. I could not believe that he was placated by my satisfaction. I did not love, yes, I hated the righteous God who punishes sinners, and secretly, if not blasphemously, certainly murmuring greatly, I was angry with God, and said, 'As if, indeed, it is not enough, that miserable sinners, eternally lost through original sin, are crushed by every kind of calamity by the law of the decalogue, without having God add pain to pain by the gospel and also by the gospel threatening us with his righteousness and wrath!' Thus I raged with a fierce and troubled conscience. Nevertheless, I beat importunately upon Paul at that place, most ardently desiring to know what St. Paul wanted. At last, by the mercy of God, meditating day and night, I gave heed to the context of the words, namely, 'In it the righteousness of God is revealed, as it is written, "He who through faith is righteous shall live."' There I began to understand that the righteousness of God is that by which the righteous lives by a gift of God, namely by faith. And this is the meaning: the righteousness of God is revealed by the gospel, namely, the passive righteousness with which merciful God justifies us by faith, as it is written, 'He who through faith is righteous shall live.' Here I felt that I was altogether born again and had entered paradise itself through open gates. There a totally other face of the entire Scripture showed itself to me. Thereupon I ran through the Scriptures from memory. I also found in other terms an analogy, as the work of God, that is, what God does in us, the power of God, with which he makes us strong, the wisdom of God, with which he makes us wise, the strength of God, the salvation of God, the glory of God. And I extolled my sweetest word with a love as great as the hatred with which I had before hated the word 'righteousness of God.' Thus that place in Paul was for me truly the gate to paradise."

Since Luther's study, the site of this decision, was probably located in the tower of the Black Monastery, this event has been called the "tower experience." Since evidence of this newly gained interpretation of the Scriptures appeared relatively soon thereafter in the lectures on the Psalms which he was then giving, it is also possible to establish with some degree of certainty the date when it occurred: sometime during the winter semester 1512-1513 or in the spring of 1513.

This was the hour in which the Reformation was born. Without the tower experience there would have been neither the *Ninety-five Theses* nor the Diet of Worms. A whole new era had its point of departure in the struggle of an individual's search for God.

The first quiet years following his achievement of these insights were like a spiritual springtime. The shadows of fame still had not loomed up between him and the world. The new assurance poured copiously and powerfully into his disputations and lectures on the epistles to the Romans and the Galatians. A new era had been born, but for several years all that happened was that a theological world view underwent a change because a Christian man had been redeemed from his inner trials by the liberating realization of God's grace in Christ.

Some of Luther's finest treatises and disputations now came into existence. The *Ninety-five Theses* of October 31, 1517, were preceded by other theses from September of the same year, which, while in form and title they were directed against the theology of Scholasticism, in their content were fully characterized by the newly bestowed comfort of God's grace, and thus became instrumental in renewing the methodology of theology. The same new note could be heard in several letters from those early days. And beyond that historic watershed which overnight made him the most famous man in Germany, namely, the *Ninety-five Theses*, the lustre of those early days was carried forward into another set of theses, which theologically were probably the most significant of that day—the Heidelberg Disputation of 1518. In them the theological revelation which resulted from Luther's new and fundamental insight now stood in bold relief: "True theology and the knowledge of God are to be found only in Jesus Christ the Crucified."

127

Contemporary circular dealing with Tetzel's indulgence business.

When one compares Luther's tower experience with his sensational declaration in the *Ninety-five Theses,* it is immediately clear that the new era was born in the tower room of the Black Monastery at Wittenberg, and that God's hidden presence in history had manifested itself with particular clarity.

The Indulgence Controversy

Luther and many others had long been disturbed by the business of indulgences, the transformation of penance—that most profound and salutary experience of man as he stands before God, as Luther himself had undergone it in his tower experience—into a commercial transaction. In addition to his professorship he also served as pastor of the Wittenberg congregation, and in this capacity he was confronted ever more frequently with the ugly consequences of this practice. When he insisted on the need of true repentance, he was shown the little slips of paper which entitled a person to purchase penance and indulgences, that is, dispensation from the so-called penalties of hell and purgatory. It was then that he decided to take action. He had in mind not a public protest, with its noisy tumult, but rather something resembling an academic approach. In order to bring clarity to ideas held popularly within the church he chose the method of a scholarly disputation about the power and efficacy of indulgences. As yet indulgences did not belong to that category of issues which had been "defined" by Catholic dogma, that is, they had not been affirmed as binding on the believer. Thus, every academic instructor was free to deal with them in theological discussions. Luther, therefore, composed a set of theses and in accord with academic tradition issued an invitation to a discussion on them. Since the discussion was intended for theologians and churchmen, the theses appeared in Latin.

"And these he posted publicly on the church which is adjacent to the castle at Wittenberg, on the day before the Feast of All Saints in the year 1517." This is how Melanchthon described the event in 1546 in his foreword to the second volume of Luther's Latin Writings. In other words, Luther had no intention of acting in a manner that would, so to speak, exclude the public. It was to the academic community to which he turned and it was the proper churchly approach that he used.

Not a single person appeared at the time announced for the disputation. For about a fortnight a deathly silence surrounded the Theses. But this was only the brief span of time that elapsed between the spark and the explosion.

Then the tempest broke loose. After some hesitation Luther had sent a copy to some of his friends. Completely without his approval and probably against his will these friends arranged for the circulation of the Theses and with great rapidity the Theses were circulated throughout Germany. As a sign of his approval, no less a person than Albrecht Dürer at that time sent a number of woodcuts and engravings to the monk who was a complete stranger to him. Countless others thought as he did. The storm swept through Germany with such momentum that it startled even Luther.

Suddenly he began to realize that by his action he had undertaken nothing less than to "assault the heavens and set the world on fire." The stronger the response became and the greater the influence exerted by the Theses, the more he became aware of the historic struggle that was building up: "The song tended to become too high for my voice." The ultimate result of this single act which had emanated from Luther's conscientious theological and pastoral concern as well as from his newly acquired biblical insight, was the very thing which he never intended or anticipated: the inspiration for a decisive turning point in history.

In order to understand this clearly, it is now necessary to clarify two matters.

Through all these events Luther simply followed his own personal path of obedience to faith. The insight about the nature of God's grace and about divine forgiveness to which his tower experience had brought him was incompatible both in principle and practice with what had happened to the idea of penance at the hands of the indulgence peddlers. With an amazing clarity he developed his theological repudiation of these abuses, but he did it in such a way that every aspect of religiousness, indeed, even the entire dogma of salvation as held by the medieval church, was dealt a decisive blow. And because Luther's Theses unexpectedly exercised an extensive and widespread influence, his attack achieved a greater prominence than that achieved by reform efforts undertaken in the past. Basically his historic act grew out of his own religious experience. He had not deliberately set out to perform some historic act. Not a single one of his acts was undertaken because he aspired to power. All his life he demonstrated a lofty contempt for power, because from a human point of view he was a genius who did not require the external means of naked power. Actually, he had no need of force because his faith in God's providential leading within this world determined everything which he did. Only because he was obedient to the insights into truth granted him by God did he set out upon the road which determined the course of history.

Rome's initial disregard of this historic upheaval is rather perplexing. It is possibly of little importance that Luther's good but probably very insignificant bishop of Brandenburg, could see no reason to interfere. This bishop instead confined his response to a harmless but well-intentioned written word of approval when Luther dutifully first informed him of his action. Similarly unimportant is the fact that the person primarily affected, the very busy and prosperous Albrecht of Mainz, whom Luther had also immediately and dutifully notified, had left it up to his councilors to proceed in the manner popular among secular and ecclesiastical chanceries, namely, to allow Luther's communication to lie unread on someone's desk. But the fact that it took so long for Rome to grasp the far-reaching significance of this event was and remains astonishing. Actually it was not until 1518 at Augsburg that Rome made the initial effort through Cardinal Cajetan to bring about a theological discussion with Luther. One really cannot avoid the impression that Rome's delay in acting was evidence that Rome was ripe for the judgment of history, in the course of which half of Europe was to turn away from it.

Luther at Heidelberg

The present Street of the Augustinians was once—as the detail from the engraving by Merian shows—the location of the Augustinian Monastery in whose lecture hall the Heidelberg Disputation took place between April 21 and May 1, 1518. For the later reformers of southern Germany, such as Brenz, Schnepf, and Bucer, this event became the crucial hour in their lives and a milestone in the forward movement of the Reformation.

Heidelberg, showing the university, St. Peter's Church and the Augustinian Monastery, detail from the copper engraving by Matthew Merian.

Luther before Cajetan, a contemporary book illustration.

The Hearing at Augsburg

Six months after the Heidelberg Disputation and as a sequel to a very involved bit of political maneuvering Luther was given an informal hearing before Cardinal Cajetan, papal legate to the 1518 session of the diet held in Augsburg. Luther's phenomenal command of the language is revealed in the final confrontation with Cajetan, the conclusion of which Luther describes as follows: "Then I— in disrespect, to be sure—burst out in anger: 'Don't get the idea, most reverend father, that we Germans are ignorant in the field of grammar. "To be a treasure" and to "gain a treasure" are two different things!' At that point his hopes were shattered, even though he continued to shout that I should recant. As I walked away, he called after me: 'Away with you—don't let me see you again unless you are ready to recant!'" Luther's fate and that of the Reformation now rested in the hands of two men: Spalatin and Frederick the Wise. Yielding in the face of what was now inevitable, Staupitz absolved Luther from his vow of obedience to the order.

133

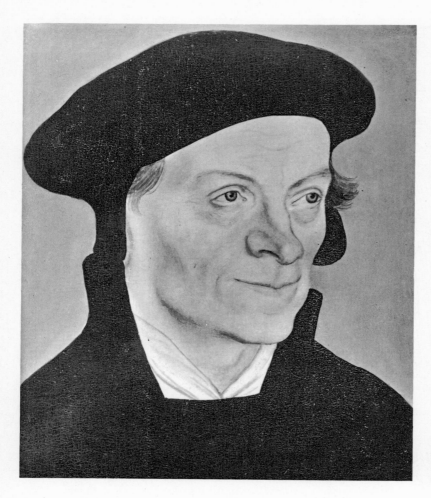

The Reformer Spalatin, a picture from the school of Lucas Cranach the Elder in 1537.

George Burkhardt of Spalt-Spalatin

Luther and Spalatin were almost the same age. In 1505 Spalatin became the instructor of novices at the Georgenthal Monastery in Thuringia; in 1508 at Torgau, tutor to a son of the heir to the throne of Electoral Saxony. Due to his humanistic, theological, and legal knowledge he soon became private secretary to Elector Frederick the Wise. He served as liaison between the sovereign and the university and in all matters that pertained to Luther. Electoral Saxony's vigorous and successful support of Luther must be attributed largely to the sagacity of Spalatin.

134

Frederick the
Wise, 1524
copper
engraving by
Albrecht Dürer.

Frederick the Wise

Among the royalty of that day this monarch was truly unique. His decisions were motivated neither by the cool, calculating reasons of state, nor by the urge for power, nor by personal ambition, but by the concerned conscience of a sovereign who knew that he was responsible to God. He never spoke with Luther himself and sent only one letter in Luther's behalf to the Curia. This one letter of December 18, 1518, however, contains his refusal to hand Luther over to Rome. He writes, "If we were convinced that his teaching is impious and untenable we would not defend him. Our sole objective is to conduct our affairs like a Christian prince."

D: Diui Maximiliani Romanorum Cesaris Christiana vita Et feliciffimo eius obitu ꝛc Ad Reuerendiffimū in Christo patrem et illustrem Principem Fabriciū de Car-
reto ꝛ Marchionibus finalis facrofancte domꝰ ta Hospitalis fancti Joannis Hierofolimitani Militaris ordinis Magnum magistrum Rhodi ꝛc vt precipuū Cesaris obfequenfi Jacobi
Manlij doctoris eiufdem ordinis in Germania Cancellarij ꝛ dicti Cesaris hiftoriographi apud Mesfana.
Debis quibus potiffime iam corpore egrotante animū reficiebat Cesar.

Cesari antiquiffime et nobiliffime Genealogie
eius per Manlium libri leguntur.

De feliciffimo Cesaris obitu et exanimi corpore sub Crucifixi et Mi-
litaribus s. Georgii infignibus ad Sarcophagū depofito

Cum priuilegio Imperiali.

John Eck, professor
at the University of
Ingolstadt, copper
engraving by
Peter Weinher
the Elder.

New Turn of Events

With the refusal of Elector Frederick the Wise to comply with the extradition demands of the pope, Luther, at the end of 1518, had his first opportunity to regain his breath. Then in January of 1519 Emperor Maximilian died. The election of a new emperor was now completely in the foreground. However, the theological discussions continued concurrently. While the electors were choosing a new emperor in the summer of 1519 an eagerly awaited debate with Dr. John Eck, professor of theology at Ingolstadt, took place in Leipzig. A skilled debater, Eck succeeded in getting Luther to expose himself even more than heretofore. Now the church needed no further clarification in its effort to establish its position. The decision pressed on toward its climax.

O Carle / Keyßer lobesan /
greiff du die sach zům erſten an /
Gott würts mit dir on zweyfel hatt.

On the right page:
Luther with the doc-
tor's hat, 1521
engraving by
Lucas Cranach
the Elder.

Contemporary picture
portraying Charles V at
the time of his election,
from a pamphlet written
by Ulrich von Hutten.

The Election of Charles V

*When on June 28, 1519, the bells of Frankfurt proclaimed the election
of Charles I of Spain as the German emperor, a stubborn behind-
the-scenes game of political and financial intrigue had come to an end.
The only serious opposition candidate was Frederick the Wise,
but, recognizing clearly that in the impending bloody European and
internal German conflicts his royal house would have lacked the power to
muster a decisive counterforce, he had withdrawn his candidacy at
the last moment. Now the young emperor and the Doctor—as Cranach
portrayed him in those days—stood opposed to each other.*

138

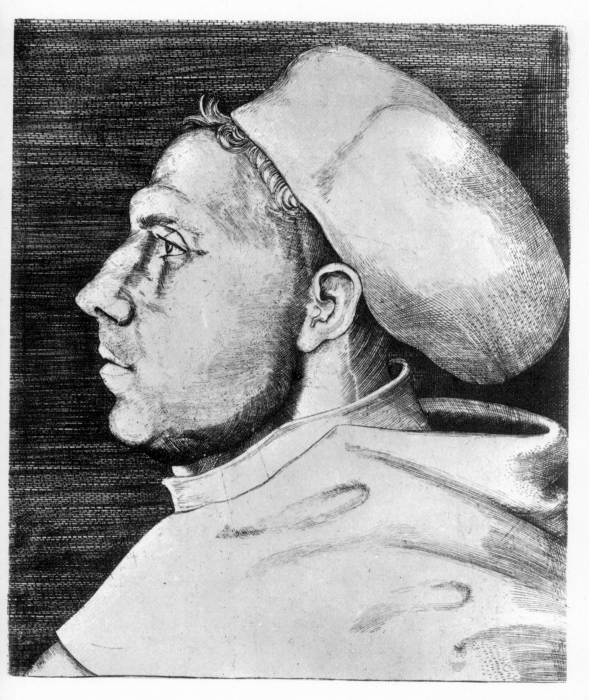

139

Von der Freyhayt
Aines Christen
menschen.

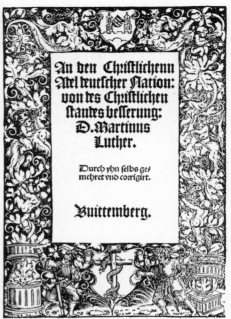

An den Christlichenn
Adel deutscher Nation:
von des Christlichen
standes besserung:
D. Martinus
Luther.

Durch yhn selbs ge=
mehret vnd corrigirt.

Buittemberg.

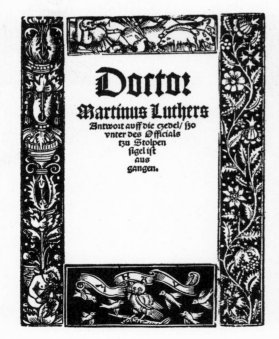

Doctor
Martinus Luthers
Antwort auff die czedel/ so
vnter des Officials
tzu Stolpen
sigel ist
aus
gangen.

Ein sermon von dem
hochwirdigen sacrament des heyligen
waren leichnamß Christi. Vnd von den bruderschafften. D.M.L.A.

Fur die Leyen.

On the left page: Title pages from Luther's writings of the years 1519 and 1520.

The Freedom of a Christian, printed 1520 at Hagenau by Thomas Anschelm.

To the Christian Nobility of the German Nation, printed 1520 at Wittenberg by Melchior Lotter.

Doctor Martin Luther's Answer to the Statement Issued over the Seal of the Chancery of Stolberg, printed 1520 at Leipzig by Valentine Schumann.

A Sermon on the Blessed Sacrament of the Holy and True Body of Christ, printed 1519 at Nürnberg by Jobst Gutknecht.

On the right: Title page of the papal bull of January 3, 1521, against the errors of Luther.

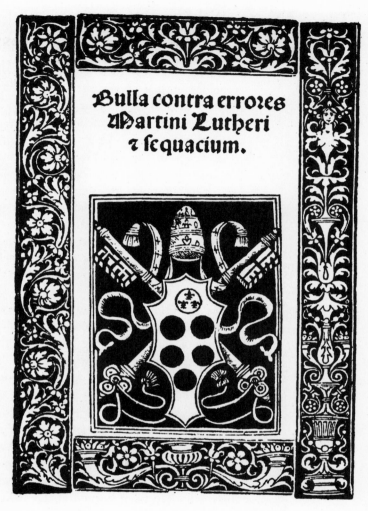

Check and Countercheck

*The year 1520 produced two important, preclimactic events:
first, the papal bull issued on June 15 which threatened Luther
with excommunication and which reached him in October; second,
the publication of four of his own polemical writings in which
he no longer restricted himself to the issue of penance and
indulgences but called for the reformation of the church in its
entirety, and called upon the nobility of the realm to go over the
head of the pope and hand in hand with a general council of
the church to initiate and execute the reformation of the church.*

The Diet of Worms

There are but few instances when a climax in the history of the world coincides with a climax in the history of the church. This happened on April 17 and 18 in the year 1521 at the Diet of Worms. This day marked a significant turning point in history.

What was this day like?

Anyone who happened to be in Worms on April 16, 1521, could not help but sense that something significant was in the offing. This medium-sized city of about seven thousand inhabitants was crowded with visitors. On hand were the young emperor, the object of at least friendly curiosity on the part of the people, and the princes of the realm. Present also was the papal nuncio Aleander, one of the few men fully aware of the implications of the event, who in his excitement dispatched innumerable reports in quick succession to Rome, thereby furnishing us with details which while copious are not always reliable.

The attention of the public, however, was focused not on these men but on Martin Luther. People had followed the news of the triumphant journey of the Wittenberg friar through the German lands. Many knew that protracted diplomatic maneuvers had revolved around the question whether Luther was even to come in order to appear before the emperor and the empire, but only a few were aware of the tenacity with which Luther's wise Elector had fought for and finally succeeded in securing a hearing for Luther in person. Up to the very last minute the papists had done everything in their power to thwart the personal presence of the Wittenberg Augustinian at Worms. Unmistakable threats had been made, and the people had not forgotten the fate that befell the unfortunate John Huss, who had been burned at the stake in Constance despite the imperial letter of safe-conduct. And then when Luther, despite all these considerations and with a magnificent confidence, still undertook the journey, the people admired the courage of his faith with glowing enthusiasm. People passed on the words that he had spoken: "Even if they kindled a fire between Wittenberg and Worms that reaches up to the heavens," because he had been summoned, he would still appear in the name of the Lord, would "tread into the behemoth's maw between its huge teeth, and would confess Christ and let him have his way." It was known that he had rejected a note of warning sent to him at the last moment by the court preacher of his own elector: "Even if there were as many devils in Worms as there are tiles on the roofs, I would surely enter the city."

Thus, as even his contemporaries already reported, this journey turned into a triumphal procession. Erfurt University's faculty, with the rector at its head, had welcomed him at the city gates with pomp as though he were a prince. On Misericordias Domini Sunday he preached on the Gospel for the day in the overcrowded church of his order. An eyewitness reports that the church was so packed "that the balcony began to creak and everyone thought that it would collapse. Some of the people in the balcony broke windows and would have jumped down into the churchyard if Luther had not consoled them and told them to remain still since the devil was just making his ghastly noises, and if they remained quiet no evil would befall them—and there was no accident." The sermon, which has been preserved, may be regarded as typical of Luther's inner attitude and sermonic activity during the entire journey. He was concerned above all with the gospel of God's outpoured grace, and it is only very parenthetically that one comes across a sentence that refers to the historic reason for his journey: "I know well that one does not like to hear this. Nevertheless I shall speak the truth, and I must do it even if it costs me a score of necks, for they shall not be able to condemn me."

Early in the morning of April 16, a large number of noblemen had ridden out to meet him, and servants of the city council had their hands full keeping the crowds in check when the trumpet signal from the tower of the cathedral sounded, as was customary when important visitors were announced. For now—it was about ten o'clock in the forenoon—Luther entered the city like a conquering hero. Casper Sturm, the imperial herald, bearer of the imperial letter of safe-conduct, rode ahead of the little carriage with its protective roof in which Luther, with three other companions, had made the long journey. Only with difficulty could he make his way through the crowds that numbered in the thousands.

It is necessary to take a critical look at the prevalent popular mood with which the crowds greeted Luther. The crowds undoubtedly were motivated by a composite of curiosity, enthusiasm, and sensationalism. Were all these people who lined the streets Christians seized by the fervor of a new revival? To assume such a thing would be naive. For untold numbers Luther was the focal point of the steadily growing national consciousness, which, although still torpid, was always present beneath the surface. When Erasmus, during his German trip a few years earlier, had traveled along the Rhine, there had been a great display of enthusiasm, and he accepted it with a certain amount of astonishment. He knew better than the easily enthused Germans that he did not deserve such displays of enthusiasm. This national sentiment discovered its true object in Luther, and if one is aware of this, then it seems that those who regard the Reformation primarily as a movement are correct. Certainly it is true that there were probably few days in the history of Germany when national sentiment erupted as spontaneously as on this day at Worms. Nonetheless, one must not overlook the fact that this sentiment had its roots in the concerns of a religious faith.

Luther appeared twice before the diet. Late in the afternoon of April 17 he made his appearance at the episcopal palace in the courtroom with the low ceiling. About four o'clock the imperial marshal Ulrich von Pappenheim and the imperial herald Casper Sturm had called for him and, because of the huge throngs in the streets, had led him through secret passageways to the episcopal headquarters where the diet was in session. It was not until six o'clock that his matter was brought before the diet for discussion and with it the moment when he truly and literally faced "the emperor and the empire." The first meeting, however, was brief and formal, and the hour had little historical significance. A number of contemporary portraits, however, help us to see the two major personalities: Charles V and Luther. The youthful emperor was well aware that it would be his life calling "to stake his kingdoms and seigniories, his friends, his body and blood, his life and soul . . . in defense of the Catholic faith and the Roman church." For this reason he could regard Luther as nothing but a heretic whose profoundest concern he understood as little as his language. At that time this young emperor was more pale than in later years, and his Hapsburg chin was protruded more than in later years when his person bore the unmistakable dignity of imperial royalty. But Lucas Cranach's copper engraving of Luther in the year 1521 portrays a strong profile, a firm brow, powerfully arched eyebrows, and a determined chin and mouth. No painter's brush has ever been able to reproduce that which was most striking about his face: the brightness of his dark eyes, considered by some to be demonic, by others radiant. A contemporary mentions that his eyes "flashed and sparkled like a star so that it was not quite possible to look at them."

But the emissaries of the foreign powers who, like many of the German princes, now saw the world-renowned Augustinian friar from Wittenberg for the first time, were disappointed. The secretary of the Archbishop of Treves, Dr. John Eck, had been instructed to ask Luther two questions:

whether he acknowledged authorship of the books that lay before him, and whether he was ready to retract them, either in part or as a whole. After the titles of the books had been ascertained Luther answered the first of the two questions in the affirmative. In the case of the second, he requested additional time for reflection, a request which could not very well be denied him. Having been notified that on the following day he would be expected to give his answer, freely and without a manuscript, he was at once escorted outside. Since he—presumably upon the advice of the Elector of Saxony or his councilors—had spoken very softly in order not to appear to be ill-mannered, it is not surprising that those who were less well-disposed toward him felt that he had been overawed, and that the adversaries in general, who had been "almost thunder-struck" by his intrepid willingness to come in the first place, immediately began to think that this affair would be settled quickly and without difficulty.

In view of the constantly increasing throngs, the great hall of the episcopal palace had been chosen as the site of the next day's proceedings, but again the crowd was so great that even the princes had to stand. The hearing began about six o'clock in the evening and since it had already gotten dark, the torches were lighted. Again Dr. Eck opened the hearing and this time Luther gave a detailed answer to the second question whether he was prepared to retract parts of his books. His address was brief, clear, and was spoken in a strong voice and in German. It probably lasted no longer than ten minutes. He was then asked to repeat the address immediately in Latin. He acknowledged that the books were his, and divided them into three groups: devotional writings, books directed against the papacy, and polemical writings against individuals. He stated that no one could be interested in his retraction of the first group. But he was likewise unable to retract his writings against the papal tyranny, which had caused such great suffering to the "most renowned German nation." The same applied to the third group. But he requested everyone by the mercy of God and on the basis of the Holy Scriptures to convince him of a better truth wherever he might be in error. Only in this way could the schism of which he was being accused be overcome.

Since this address expressed not only a blunt rejection but also the readiness to be reasoned with on the basis of Scripture, the princes, who went into caucus immediately thereafter, found themselves in a difficult situation. They could not simply refuse to take cognizance of his offer, but still less could they agree to a religious disputation on issues which, according to the official position of the church, had already been refuted. The emperor especially was not willing to do so. The result was a compromise resolution to ask Luther once again whether he was willing to recant. When at the plenary session Eck repeated the question, Luther gave the answer which has made him and the Diet of Worms so famous. Speaking in Latin he said:

"Since then your serene majesty and your lordships seek a simple answer, I will give it in this manner, neither horned nor toothed: Unless I am convinced by the testimony of the Scriptures or by clear reason—for I do not trust either in the pope or in councils alone, since it is well-known that they have often erred and contradicted themselves—I am bound by the Scriptures I have quoted and my conscience is captive to the Word of God. I cannot and I will not retract anything, *since it is neither safe nor right to go against conscience.*" Then he added in German the brief entreaty of the lansquenets with which he was in the habit of often concluding his sermons—probably because he was aware of the consequences of his refusal: "God help me, Amen."

When, following a brief verbal exchange with Dr. Eck, he soon thereafter, upon a signal from the emperor, was escorted outside, a sudden tumult arose among the pressing crowds because some of the noblemen thought he had been arrested and was to be taken to a dungeon. When Luther spoke to them and calmed them, they happily fell in behind him, and, as was customary after a victory in a jousting tournament, raised their arms high and spread their fingers. Luther did the same thing when he returned to his quarters in St. John's Court, and joyfully exclaimed, "I've made it, I've made it!"

That was the Diet of Worms as posterity has remembered it.

To stop there, however, would be to overlook the fact that for Luther the several days that followed were much more demanding than the two days of the trial. For now private negotiations and conferences behind the scenes were begun, all with the single objective of somehow persuading Luther to yield. Since a number of the men involved in these efforts were honorable and scholarly individuals, since the approach to Luther was based not on imperiousness but on persuasion, and since the pressures of power politics also came to the fore with the ever-familiar reasoning among realistic politicians that unity must be maintained under all circumstances, it was not easy for Luther to maintain his position, especially since in all these discussions he was basically left as much on his own as during the two days of the trial. But in all this maneuvering the two main figures— Martin Luther and the emperor—remained adamant. Thus the final stage, which had more and more become inevitable, was reached: On April 25 Dr. Eck, accompanied by the imperial secretary Siebenbürger, appeared at St. John's Court to inform Luther (in Latin and on orders from the emperor) that since all admonitions had been to no avail the emperor, as the patron of the church, would have to take action against him. The letter of safe-conduct would be valid for an additional three weeks, but he would immediately have to put an end to his preaching and writing. Having withdrawn for a few moments into the solitude of prayer, Luther then responded with a word of gratitude to the emperor and the estates of the realm for having listened to him. He was prepared to suffer all things—even death and total dishonor—for the emperor and the empire. But he would always have to insist on his right to proclaim freely and bear witness to the Word of God.

On the following day, the morning of April 26, Luther and his companions quietly departed from Worms in two carriages through the town gate of St. Martin.

On the way home he was "waylaid" near Eisenach by troopers from Electoral Saxony and taken to Wartburg Castle. Here he was to be protected from hostile forces, and at the same was to be allowed that sublime leisure out of which blossomed one of the loveliest fruits of his entire life's labors—the translation of the Holy Scriptures, of the New Testament.

The citation issued by
Charles V in 1521 summoning
Luther to Worms.

Worms, detail from a book illustration by Sebastian Münster.

Emperor Charles V, a portrait painted shortly before the Diet of Worms.

150

The emperor's pass
of safe-conduct
issued to Luther.

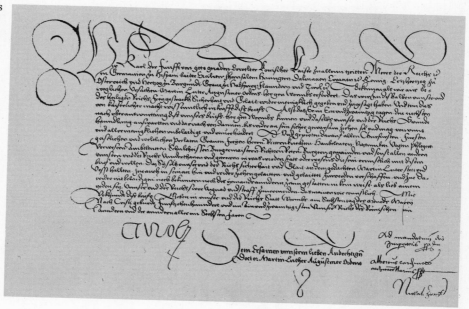

Cardinal Jerome Aleander,
engraving by Agostino Veneziano.

Frederick the Wise, copper
engraving by Lucas Cranach
the Elder.

Cardinal Albrecht of Brandenburg, detail
from a copper engraving by Albrecht Dürer.

Franz von Sickingen, detail from
a contemporary woodcut.

The Declaration of the Emperor

On the day following Luther's appearance, Charles V, fully aware of
the seriousness of the hour and of his own majesty, on his own
initiative and with his own hand wrote out the following declaratory
decree: "You know that I am descended from the most Christian
emperors of the noble German nation, from the Catholic kings of
Spain . . . all of whom remained faithful sons of the Roman church
even to their deaths, and were defenders of the Catholic faith, the
sacred rituals . . . who after death left all that to us by natural right
and heritage . . . and as true followers of these our predecessors
we have lived up to now. . . . I am determined to support everything laid
down by my predecessors since the Council of Constance. For it is
certain that a single friar errs in his opinion which is against all
Christendom and according to which all of Christianity will be and
will always have been in error for a thousand years. . . . I am no
longer willing to hear him speak. . . . Let him have his safe-conduct. . . .
I am determined hereafter to regard him as a notorious heretic. . . ."

The imperial herald Casper Sturm, drawing by Albrecht Dürer in the diary of his Netherlands journey.

Dürer's Lament

When Luther was waylaid near Eisenach and abducted, no one knew that this had been staged on orders from Frederick in order to protect him from the murderous intentions of a third party. Albrecht Dürer confided to his diary how shocked people were when news of Luther's disappearance spread. Dürer writes, "Whether he lives, or whether they have murdered him—which I do not know—he has suffered this for the sake of the Christian truth. . . . O God, if Luther is dead, who will now present the Gospel to us so clearly! O God, to think of what he might have been able to write for us in another ten or twenty years! O all you good Christian people, help me diligently to bewail this God-inspired man."

Luther as Knight Jörg, with the city of Worms in the background, a symbolical picture by Heinrich Göding commemorating Luther's stay at the Wartburg Castle (woodcut).

155

Luther as Knight Jörg,
painted by Lucas Cranach
the Elder during Luther's
brief stay at Wittenberg,
December 5-10, 1521.

Knight Jörg

*Luther had this to say about his protective custody at the
Wartburg: "Then I was pulled out of the carriage and
set on a horse. The horsemen make some evasive moves
and take all kinds of detours in order to lead the pursuers
astray. They spend all day doing this. At night I arrive
on the Wartburg near Eisenach. From there I often
climbed down to go hunting like a junker, gathered straw-
berries, even met with the Franciscans, but all was done in
secret. That's how well the troopers can hold their tongues!"*

richte mich herre vnd fure mir meine sache. vnd
der das vnruhiglige rede

vnd errette mich von den falschen vnd bösen leuten
denn du bist der gott meyner stercke warumb verstossestu
warumb lessestu mich so traurig gehen weil mich dranget
weil mich der feyndt

Sende deyn liecht vnd deyne warheit das sie mich leyten
vnd bringen zu deynem heyligen berge vnd zu deyner wo
das ich hyneyn gehe zum altar gottes zu dem gott
meyner freuden wonne, vnd dir danck der harffe dancke
Gott meyn gott

Was betrubestu dich meyne seele vnd bist so vnruhig yn mir
harre auff gott, denn ich werde yhm noch dancken das das
heyl seynes angesichts

Eyn unterweisung der kinder Korah vorzusingen.

Gott wir haben mit unsern oren gehort, unser veter
habens uns erzelet, was du than hast zu yhren zey
ten vor alters

Du hast mit deyner hand die heyden vertrieben und sie geschleudert
du hast die volcker verterbet und sie außgestossen

Denn sie haben das land nicht eingenomen durch yhr schwerd
vnd yhr arm halff yhn nicht

Sondern deyne rechte, deyn arm vnd das liecht deyns angesichts
denn du hattest gefallen an yhnen
Du bist meyn konig gott
befilh hilff Jacob zu richten
ir du gebeutest

St. Jerome in his study, picture by Master A. W. in a later edition of the "September Testament" from the years 1532 and 1535.

On the left: Luther's manuscript of Psalm 43 from his translation of the Bible.

Luther at Study

Less than ten days after his capture Luther was again at work. On May 14 he writes to Spalatin, "Here I was stripped of my own clothes and dressed in a knight's cloak. I am letting my hair and beard grow, so that you would hardly know me; I can't even recognize myself any longer. Now I am living in Christian liberty and am free of all the laws of the tyrant. . . . I am reading the Bible in Greek and Hebrew. I shall write a German tract on the freedom of auricular confession. I shall continue working on the Psalms and the Postil. . . ."

The New Testament in German

Separated from his friends and his congregation, Luther, in the solitude of the Wartburg, began the great task of the future: the orderly structuring of evangelical life. In addition to devotional writings and passionate tracts provoked by the polemics of his opponents, he was busy at two important labors: the so-called Church Postil, a collection of model sermons aimed at raising the low level of preaching; second, the start on the translation of the book basic to all evangelical life— the New Testament. He labored almost entirely without the use of any resource materials. Yet in three months he had completed the almost impossible task. It is a philological and linguistic accomplishment whose influence has been felt through the centuries.

Title page of a booklet dealing with a dialogue between two peasants—Karsthans and Kegelhans—concerning Luther's path of suffering, printed at Strassburg in 1521.

New Struggles Begin

As early as the summer of 1521 it was apparent that it would become necessary to distinguish between the Reformation concept slowly developed by Luther on the basis of his religious experience, and the spontaneous reactions unleashed by the forces at work within the social structure of that day. Luther rejected identification with the easily aroused emotions. No human interference was necessary to ensure the progress of the Reformation. The Word of God alone provided the guidelines. But in certain matters where external guidance was required, such guidance was to be provided by the secular authorities. Should they fail in their duties, then the established forms of the past were to be observed, for the order of the medieval worship service could also be interpreted spiritually and therefore be accepted. All undue burdens upon the consciences of individuals were to be avoided. However, events soon outdistanced the admonitions from the Wartburg. Luther's colleague at the university, Andreas Karlstadt, and Luther's radically inclined monastery companion, Gabriel Schilling, raised three questions: Were priests permitted to marry? Should monks leave the monasteries? What was to be done about the Roman mass? Along with several of his students, Melanchthon received the Lord's Supper in both kinds. Provost Bartholemew Bernhard of Kemberg took a wife. Neither the Lord's Supper nor the mass was celebrated at the Augustinian monastery. Riots broke out in December, 1521. Priests officiating at mass were driven from the altars, pictures of saints were removed, and altars were razed. Only one person could help: during the week of March 1, 1522, Luther returned to Wittenberg.

Captured peasants, woodcut from the year 1523.

Illustration of the Book of Revelation in the "September Testament," depicting the seven bowls of wrath.

Wie gar gfarlich sey. So
Ain Priester kain Ee weyb hat. Wye Vn
christlich. vnd schedlich aim gmainen
Nutz Die menschen seynd. Welche
hindern die Pfaffen Am Ee=
lichen stand. Durch
Johan Eberlin Von Güntzburg. Anno.

Title page from a 1522
circular by John Eberlin
von Güntzburg, depicting
the marriage of bishops,
monks, and nuns.

Preaching *The Eight Wittenberg Sermons against the Enthusiasts and Iconoclasts* he was able to calm the situation and regain a firm grip on the further progress of events. Karlstadt sulked, but Gabriel Schilling admitted that they had gone too far. The key thoughts expressed by Luther in these sermons were: "In short, I will preach it, teach it, write it, but I will constrain no man by force, for faith must come freely without compulsion. . . . I did nothing; the Word did everything."

Satirical woodcut of the seven-headed Martin Luther, from a polemical
tract by John Cochlaeus from the year 1529.

Die recht warhafft vñ

Gründtlich Hystori oder geschicht Von brüder Hainrich inn
Diethmar verprent/durch Martinum Lucher be=
schriben sampt dem Zehenden Psalmen auß=
gelegt zü Wittemberg: M. D. xxv.

The martyrdom of
Henry of Zütphen,
woodcut from Luther's
1525 pamphlet *The
Burning of Brother
Henry.*

*Two years of unflagging labors now followed. First there
were the journeys: Altenburg, Zwickau, Borna, Eilenburg,
Torgau, Weimar, Erfurt. In Zwickau, fourteen thousand
people came to hear Luther preach. In June of 1522 his
treatise* A Little Prayer Book of the Ten Commandments
appeared; in September, The Estate of Marriage *and the
"September Testament." Luther began work on the translation
of the Pentateuch. But the world around him was on the*

move. Monks and nuns continued to leave the monasteries. In April of 1523, Katherine von Bora, who later became Luther's wife, fled from the Nimbschen convent in Grimma with eleven other nuns. In July at Brussels two young Augustinian monks, Henry Vos and John van den Esschen, were publicly burned at the stake and became the first martyrs of the Reformation. Inspired by the events at Brussels Luther himself embarked upon his own venture as a writer of songs.

Title page of the prize ballad composed in 1523 by Hans Sachs in honor of Luther, *The Wittenberg Nightingale.*

From Luther's *Preface to All Good Hymnals*

DAME MUSIC SPEAKS:

Of all the joys on earth
The one that gives most mirth
Is when my melodies I sing
And all the world with songs does ring.
There cannot be an ugly mood
When men in song are deep renewed.
Gone then are envy, hate, and strife,
No heartache left to hurt our life.

The year's best time is always mine
When all the birds to song incline,
They crowd the earth and fill the skies
With songs that always earn the prize.
Sweet nightingale is leader there,
Brings joy to all and everywhere
With lovely lays that she keeps
   singing,
While we to her our thanks are
   bringing.

A Children's Song for the Birth of Christ

THE ANGEL SINGS

Good news from heaven the angels bring,
Glad tidings to the earth they sing:
To us this day a Child is given
To crown us with the joy of heaven.

In this arrangement of the verses of the Christmas song we follow the interpretation of George Buchwald, who thought of it as a children's nativity play in miniature.

THE ANNOUNCEMENT TO THE CHILDREN

This is the Christ, our God and Lord,
Who in all need shall aid afford;
He will Himself our Saviour be,
From all our sins to set us free.

These are the tokens ye shall mark:
The swaddling clothes and manger
   dark;
There ye shall find the Infant laid
By whom the heavens and earth were
   made.

THE CHILDREN WALK TO THE MANGER

Now let us all with gladsome cheer
Go with the shepherds and draw near
To see the precious Gift of God,
Who hath His own dear Son bestowed.

THEY GREET THE CHRIST CHILD

All hail, Thou noble Guest, this morn,
Whose love did not the sinner scorn;
In my distress Thou com'st to me;
What thanks shall I return to Thee?

Ah, Lord, who hast created all,
How weak art Thou, how poor and
   small,
That Thou dost choose Thine infant
   bed
Where humble cattle lately fed!

Were earth a thousand times as fair,
Beset with gold and jewels rare,
She yet were far too poor to be
A narrow cradle, Lord, for Thee.

THE CHILDREN CIRCLE AROUND THE MANGER

My heart for very joy doth leap,
My lips no more can silence keep;
I, too, must sing with joyful tongue
That sweetest ancient cradlesong:

Praise God upon His heavenly throne,
Who gave to us His only Son:
For this His hosts, on joyful wing,
A blest New Year of Mercy sing.

Luther as a Poet

*Luther was the most important poet of his day. His lyrical
accomplishments grew out of dual roots: in the first place,
out of the experience of his personal struggle against the dark powers
of the world, thus inspiring him toward poetic utterances; in the
second place, out of the practical considerations which imposed
themselves upon the Reformer who found himself faced with the task
of restructuring the whole life of the church. It was toward this end
that he had to create new forms for public worship. These forms
would have to define precisely the extent of the congregation's
participation and assign to it an active role. This active role becomes
especially clear in the singing of hymns by the congregation. A letter
to George Spalatin (see p. 184) conveys to us Luther's ideas on
this subject.*

Reproduction of two
pages of the hymn "A
Mighty Fortress is our
God," based on Psalm 46
and first printed in 1529
although the hymn
originated at an earlier
date.

The Year of Decision and Division: 1525

The Peasants' War

The year 1525 was the pinnacle of Luther's greatness and a turning point in his personal life and in the development of the Reformation. In his writings and in his way of life he now made the final break with the Middle Ages. 1525 was also the year of the Peasants' War. The position taken by Luther in this time of bloody rebellion, to which he gave expression in several strongly worded publications dealing with the political situation, cost him his hitherto unique popularity among the people. Thus the months of May and June of the year 1525 became the loneliest period in Luther's life.

A conscientious historical account of this period dare not whitewash Luther. The actual revolt of the peasants was presumably just as justified as later on it was inexcusable because of its excesses. The revolt began —in various localities with varying intensity—with the composition of the *Twelve Articles of the Peasants in Swabia,* a document which unfolds Christian ideas with simple dignity. The fires of rebellion would not have swept across Germany so rapidly if there had not been another even more weighty historical right in the background. The princes, who played a deplorable role throughout the course of the rebellion, were numbed with fear at first. Even later on Luther denounced their lamentable behavior with phrases which today cannot be accepted as approved literature: ". . . these same sorry fellows, who now deprive God of his honor, and who now praise themselves and boast as if they had done it all, were at that time such timid rascals, as I have never seen before in all my life. Now they forget God who rescued them at that time when they ignominiously defecated in their trousers, so that the stench still remains where one of those pathetic fellows walks or stands. At that time knighthood had neither the heart nor the courage to do what should have been done." Only at the last moment did the princes close ranks, and after inflicting a crushing defeat on the peasants in the battle of Frankenhausen on May 15, 1525, they wreaked a horrible vengeance. For a short while Germany was drenched in blood. Thomas Müntzer, a radical preacher and leader of a peasant army, was captured and beheaded.

Luther's position in these terrible conflicts has often been presented in an unfavorable light. Anyone who reflects upon the bloody episode of the Peasants' Revolt and its many aspects and then tries to sketch the men of action into this cruel picture, will always be inclined to regard Thomas Müntzer as the more consistent, and possibly to a much greater degree the more heroic man of deeds. Müntzer's claim to fame is based not only on the fact that he was the first person to conduct a mass completely in German but that he was more logical and consistent than Luther in his endeavor to apply the rule of the Bible to the political, in this instance, to the socio-revolutionary realm. We must also concede that to the very end Müntzer remained true to his convictions. And even if the last days and hours of this "theologian of rebellion" are lost to history, those reports (be they genuine or apocryphal) deserve credence that bear witness to his undaunted walk to the execution block.

How can one possibly explain Luther's attitude? For the peasants who were pressing hard for social reforms he was the intellectual leader. He had spoken to them in rather moderate language, while at the same time criticizing the princes in bitter terms. But then he had also reminded the princes in equally forceful words of what he considered to be the duties of their office, while later on always and repeatedly reproaching them for their wretched timidity. Does this not inevitably lead to the supposition that Martin Luther simply was not sure of the road to follow?

This historical verdict can best be brought into a balanced perspective if we ask the simple question: Could Luther have acted any different if he wanted to remain true to himself? He had only one guide and rule: the Word of God. Against it he appraised both the peasants and the princes.

Undoubtedly, it is one of the paramount accomplishments of Luther that on the summit of revolutionary changes he demonstrated an amazing capacity for constructive moderation. After all, he altered the form of public worship only at the one place which was crucial for him: the words of institution in the Lord's Supper were not to be spoken softly in Latin, but aloud in German, for they represented the core of his theological interpretation of the mass. Everything else remained unchanged. In all other matters of church order his decisions were based on the same principle. In those areas related more closely to public life he acted even more resolutely according to the principle which he had frequently promulgated in his sermons and public utterances, namely, that the mere destruction of the old forms is in itself not a legitimation for a historic mandate. Expressed in his own words it amounted to this: "Truly, you do not become a Christian by demolishing monasteries, by showing contempt for the authorities, or by gorging yourself with food and drink to the point of intoxication." Thus he demonstrated that an organic development was possible and by this decision determined the character of the Reformation. It cannot be denied that the radical decisions made by the enthusiasts had a more convincing and spectacular effect. But it remains indisputable that the greater historical achievement must be credited to Luther.

Luther's real tragedy lies in the fact that basically he lived on the periphery of the actual events and that in this situation he overrated the power of his statements. He followed the political events themselves with an inner fervor and an indignation that sometimes missed the mark. The most disturbing part is that what Luther had to say was composed within a definite situation and almost always arrived at its destination too late. The revolt spread faster than his ideas. It is noteworthy, however, that he remained firm in his position and faced the peasants as well as the princes with equal fearlessness. The intellectual independence from which his judgments stemmed is evidenced even years later by the manner in which he criticized the timidity, even the cowardice, of many princes who, at the proper time, should have felt themselves obligated to show both justice and mercy. In spite of the intemperateness of Luther's language, we can discern the ideal that governed him: he became pointed and sharp when he detected the clear intent to destroy the divine order. He dealt harshly with the princes when he noticed that because of their lack of courage they did not do their duty as rulers. By the same token, he interceded in behalf of the enthusiasts' right to voice their ideas, and he took up the cudgel in behalf of the right of a preacher never to remain silent when he sees an injustice. No matter what the cost might be, a preacher dare neither be silent nor give his consent to injustice. It is wrong to look upon Luther as the prophet of the authorities, or to call him (as his enemies did) the "lackey of the princes." He acted as he did in those critical years because he was convinced that he was unable to inaugurate a new political era, which was what the disorganized peasants had expected him to do. It must never be forgotten that he was one of the fathers of the European concept of tolerance, and that this "reactionary" became the spokesman for some of the basic ideas about the rights of the individual and the equality of all, and that he thereby established some of the basic principles inherent in future "European revolutions."

Luther's Marriage

His marriage to Katherine von Bora in this year of destiny calls for some special attention. The decision was made and carried out very suddenly. By taking this step, which certainly required much courage because of his prominence, Luther terminated his personal relationship to the Middle Ages, monasticism, and the legal bonds to his past. Among the reasons given by Luther for his marriage, two are paramount. He attributed it partly to his father, who, particularly after the death of his two other sons, had long ago expressed the wish that Martin Luther would marry and perpetuate the family name. His second reason was that since he had to reckon with the possibility of an early death, he looked upon his marriage in an eschatological light. The Peasants' Revolt had confirmed his feelings that he was in danger of death, and this was certainly not an exaggeration. Thus it is a sign of the boldness of his faith when, in the face of such somber eventualities, he demonstrated his affirmation of life and his acquiescence to the divine order by taking a wife. At the same time his marriage served as a testimony to others and strengthened their hesitant consciences. A note of unsentimental naturalness is added to the entire happening by the fact that—as is often true in the case of men of importance—Katherine von Bora herself, with a woman's determination, had a share in shaping Luther's decision. The theory that Luther married solely out of sexual desire is so unworthy of credence that it hardly merits a word of refutation. Militating against such a supposition are not only the conditions of the day but also Luther's relatively advanced age. He did not decide to enter the estate of matrimony until he was nearly forty-two years old. Not unimportant, however, is the personality of the woman whom Luther chose, or, as many references would lead us to surmise, chose him. Katherine von Bora, who was descended from an impoverished old family of Saxon nobility and who, with several companions, had left the convent with Luther's consent, evidently was an ideal life partner for Luther. Their marriage was characterized by that combination of affection, common sense, and fidelity which is perhaps the best prerequisite for an enduring marriage. No one ever doubted that the marriage was a happy one and that Katherine von Bora, gifted with a sober business sense, was an excellent manager of the hospitable and ever-growing household, in which the joys of music and the art of conversation reigned, and in which the master of the house was characterized by an almost prodigal generosity. Luther's numerous casual remarks in his letters and recorded in *Table Talk* prove that at the same time she was an understanding partner who shared all his spiritual problems with him.

Controversy About the Freedom of the Will

It is quite obvious that the Peasants' War and its attendant problems put Luther under a severe strain of burden. Consequently we must admire him when we realize that in spite of these trials he still possessed the intellectual vigor to write several of his finest devotional booklets and above all the monumental book on the question of the freedom of the will: In this book, *On the Bondage of the Will,* his reply to Erasmus, the prince of the Humanists, the force and fullness of Luther's thoughts poured forth like an ocean wave. He availed himself of the opportunity offered to him. Apparently with cool calculation, Erasmus had selected as a seemingly remote theological proposition for the conflict which he anticipated would result, the problem of the freedom of the will. Possibly he did this on the assumption that a polemic on this topic was not feasible and that Martin Luther would easily fall prey to his sharp-witted arguments. The manner in which Luther took up the gauntlet was simply superb. He took up the ideas of Erasmus and drove them to their logical and ultimate conclusion. Thereby at several climactic points of his book he arrived at a philosophy of history without parallel, at an interpretation of God's revelation in Christ, and thus at statements about God's salvatory will so often veiled to man in an oft incomprehensible history and in the darkness of the philosophical problems related to the freedom of the will. *On the Bondage of the Will* was Luther's most powerful, richest, and theologically most significant book.

Only life itself can write history. Events which were seemingly unrelated, crowded into the year 1525, the year of destiny. But when viewed together—the arduous conflicts occasioned by the Peasants' Revolt with the two fronts facing the peasants and the princes, his marriage, the literary labors, and the theological discussions—then once again in retrospect one can understand the judgment of Theodor Brieger: "He attains the pinnacle of his greatness."

Between the Battlelines

Totally preoccupied with the task of finding the proper form for the German mass and restructuring the worship service, Luther, at the beginning of 1524, wrote to Spalatin, who at that time was at Nürnberg awaiting the opening of the imperial diet on January 14: "In keeping with the example set by the prophets and the old church fathers, I am willing to write German Psalms for the people, so that God's Word may also abide among the people through the medium of song. I am looking everywhere for poets. Since you are so adept and gifted in the use of the German language, I ask you, too, to devote yourself to this and to adapt a Psalm into a hymn. You will have to avoid formal and uncommon expressions. Within their capacity to understand them, the people must sing words that are as simple and

Peasants execute an indulgence salesman, pen sketch by Niklaus Manuel Deutsch from the year 1525.

familiar as possible . . . and they must furthermore reproduce the meaning with transparent clarity and be as faithful to the sense of the Psalms as possible." Was Luther so enmeshed in the circles of his religious problems that he did not notice that at this very moment Germany was standing on the brink of a social revolution? What prompted him to ask Spalatin to write hymns when he was deeply involved in top-level politics in which the Reformation was the key issue? Did he not see the waves which were threatening to engulf his labors?

Luther was very well informed about matters as they stood. He observed the activities of the enthusiasts and could see how religious and socio-political ideas gradually were becoming increasingly intertwined. He experienced the first wave of the revolution, Sickingen's rebellion, that is, the rebellion of the knights, against the authority of the princes. He recognized that despite its religious camouflage this uprising was due to selfish class interests on both sides. He observed the downfall of Sickingen and the arrogance of the princes. He implored the communal authorities to take action, to establish schools, to reorganize the system of church benefices, and not merely to discard the old ways. He entered into correspondence with the Grand Master of the Teutonic Order and advised him to convert the lands of the order into a secular duchy. He admonished, scolded, and stormed, but he also gave his help when it was requested or when he was consulted. But his language became more strident and irritated. As far as he was concerned his cause was lost if he retreated but one step, if he failed to preach the gospel, and unless he succeeded in rigorously distinguishing between spiritual and secular matters. If he was successful in this endeavor, then everything else would follow naturally and logically. But if the devil won the upper hand—and by that Luther meant the inter-weaving of the religious and secular power struggles, and the economic and social thrusts of the day—then the new man whom he had discovered in the distress and struggle of his own conscience, was in the devil's power and along with him the freedom of a Christian. The Peasant's Revolt was a tragedy!

Martin Luther
in 1526,
painting by
Lucas Cranach
the Elder, now
in Stockholm.

The Year 1525

THE PEASANTS' WAR

Since December, 1524, secret gatherings of peasants have been taking place in the marsh area of the Danube. During February the mob grows in numbers from four thousand to thirty thousand.

Jan. 25 Uprising of the peasants in the Allgau region.

Feb. 9 Uprising of the peasants in the Danube marshes and along Lake Constance.

Feb. 24 Publication of the *Articles of the Allgau Peasants*. The Battle of Pavia. The victory of Charles V over Francis I of France releases German lansquenets for the Swabian Alliance. Military superiority now enables action against the peasants.

Mar. 7 "Christian Association" of the three groups (Allgau, Danube marsh area, Lake Constance) at Memmingen.

Mar. 23 Uprisings in and near Rothenburg.

Mar. 26 Uprising by peasants in the Odenwald. In the meantime the *Twelve Articles of the Swabian Peasants* have appeared in which their objectives are stated.

Apr. 1 Uprising of peasants in the Neckar Valley.

Apr. 4 Battle at Laupheim on the Danube River. Peasants defeated by Truchsess von Waldburg. The entire south from Alsace to Carinthia and the Tyrol is in revolt.

Apr. 14 Battle at Wurzach against the peasants of the Danube marshes, ending with Truchsess' victory.

Apr. 16 Atrocities by peasants at Weinsberg near Heilbronn.

Apr. 17 Truce between Truchsess and the peasants at Lake Constance. Numerical superiority of the peasants.

May 12 Battles at Böblingen and Sindelfingen against the peasants of Württemberg.

May 15 Battle at Frankenhausen in Thuringia against Thomas Müntzer, who is captured, tortured, and beheaded.

LUTHER

Jan. 1 Luther writes the first part of *Against the Heavenly Prophets in Matters of Images and Sacraments*.

Jan. 16 Journey to Torgau.

Jan. 18 Works on the second part of *Against the Heavenly Prophets*.

Feb. 2 Publishes second part of *Against the Heavenly Prophets*.

Apr. 16 Until May 4 travels through the troubled areas of Saxony and Thuringia. Plans treatise *An Admonition to Peace: a Reply to the Twelve Articles of the Peasants*.

Apr. 17 Publication of *The Abomination of the Secret Mass*.

Apr. 19 Sojourn at Eisleben. Begins work on the *Admonition*.

Apr. 20 Travels on to Stollberg. Preaches there.

Apr. 22 Sermon at Nordhausen.

Apr. 24 Sermon at Erfurt.

Apr. 25 Travels on to Weimar where he preaches.

Apr. 26 Preaches at Orlamünde.

Apr. 27 Travels to Kahla.

Apr. 28 At Jena. Writes *The Burning of Brother Henry*, a letter to the Christians at Antwerp.

May 1 Sojourn at Wallhausen. In the beginning of May he publishes *Agreement Between the Honorable Swabian Federation and the Two Peasant Groups from Lake Constance and the Allgau*, with preface and explanations by Luther.

May 19 Victory of Duke Anthony of Lorraine against the peasants of Alsace. Although safe-conduct had been promised, the unarmed peasants are slaughtered. It is estimated that eighteen thousand peasants lost their lives.

May 2 Sermon at Nordhausen. Open riots directed against Luther.

May 3 Stay at Weimar.

May 4 Stay at Seeburg. Writes *Against the Robbing and Murdering Hordes of Peasants.*

May 5 Visit to Eisleben.

May 6 At seven o'clock in the evening arrives back at Wittenberg. During the latter half of the month publishes *A Terrible Account of Thomas Münzer and of God's Judgment upon Him.*

June 13 Luther is betrothed to Katherine von Bora.

June 2 Battle at Königshofen along the Tauber River against the Franconian peasants. Victory won by Truchsess and the Electors of Treves and the Palatinate allied with him.

June 4 Battles at Ingolstadt and Sulzdorf. The defeat of the peasants is complete and final.

July 1 *An Open Letter Concerning the Hard Book against the Peasants* is published. Luther adheres adamantly to his position.

Rebellious peasants floating the Banner of the Shoe surround a knight, a book illustration from the year 1539.

Title page of
Luther's *Treatise
on Usury*, printed
at Augsburg
in 1520.

The Turning Point

*The conflicts of the Peasants' Revolt were the
heaviest burden that Luther had to shoulder since
the days of Worms. Unless he was willing to
become unfaithful to himself and his teachings,
he had to persist in his conviction. The
peasants of Germany at that time were not in
a position to restructure the social fabric within
the empire of that day. As far as its objectives
and its leadership were concerned, the
revolution remained unclear. The territorial
princes were bound to be victorious. More and
more now Luther's cause became identified
with the secular regional authorities and with
the church establishment.*

Title page of
Luther's treatise
*Against the Robbing
and Murdering
Hordes of Peasants*,
printed at Nürnberg
in 1525.

The Bond of Marriage

In one of the Table Talks Luther is quoted as relating that it was not until 1523 (research has dated it October, 1524) that he finally laid aside his monk's cowl and that he had found it difficult to take this step. His father had repeatedly asked him to do so. From then on it was his father who had pressed him to get married. Even though his friends and colleagues were marrying, Luther realized that a similar decision on his part would arouse a different and more critical reaction. The Peasants' War, the hostility and the hatred which even believers of the gospel felt toward him made him realize that he now stood between two opposing battlelines. A full understanding of his teachings and his personal position within them was now clear to him: The break with tradition had been made, that which was new had now begun. His marriage to Katherine von Bora was the seal affirming this confession.

Baptism, with Philip Melanchthon officiating, painting by Lucas Cranach the Elder on the left wing of the Wittenberg altar.

Katherine von Bora had been born January 29, 1499. After attending the monastery school at Brehna she went to live with the Cistercian nuns at Nimbschen near Grimma in 1508. It was there that in 1515 at the age of 16 years she was consecrated a nun. During Easter night, April 4-5, 1523, she fled from the convent with eleven other nuns. Luther had knowledge of the planned flight and approved it.

Katherine von Bora, Luther's wife, from the school of Lucas Cranach the Elder.

Preacher—Teacher—Counselor: 1526-1534

The Reformation reached its climax with the dramatic developments and decisions of the year 1525. But even during the years that lay ahead, between 1526 and 1534, it will be necessary to continue to distinguish between the theological labors of Luther, the activity of the friends and coworkers intimately associated with him, the actions of the emperor and the pope, as well as of their respective agencies and councilors.

Luther had not yet uttered the final divisive word, namely, his "Accordingly, we are and remain eternally divided and opposed the one to the other." This statement was not spoken until the year 1537 as a kind of last testament of Luther in the *Smalcald Articles*.

Within the camp of the Reformation there still lay ahead the confrontation and controversy with Zwingli and the south Germans, as well as the negotiations leading to the organization of the Smalcald League, the military alliance of the Evangelical estates. In the more distant future there awaited still the clarification of the relationship to Calvin, since this reformer—younger than Luther by a generation—did not emerge publicly and prominently until the publication of his dogmatic opus *The Institutes of the Christian Religion* in 1536, and especially since this work did not receive its final form and refine its point of view over against that of Lutheranism until much later.

Luther's break with Erasmus came toward the end of the first stage of the Reformation. It came about as a result of the publication of Luther's work *On the Bondage of the Will* in December of 1525. This writing was a transition to the new stage of the Reformation and is considered by many to be Luther's most profound and significant work. It represented Luther's disavowal of the uncommitted reform attempts of a Renaissance scholar, of a personal and immediate form of religion based on the philological and philosophical ideas of antiquity, and of the endeavor to incorporate a subjective Humanism into the fabric of the church. When Erasmus in his treatise directed against Luther, *The Freedom of the Will*, tried to salvage his faith in human reason and in the external and ethical progress of mankind, Luther, in rebuttal, asserted the following: "If we do not want to drop this term (free will) altogether—which would really be the safest and most Christian thing to do—we may still in good faith teach people to use it to credit man with 'free will' with respect not to what is above him, but to what is below him. That is to say, man should realize that in regard to his money and possessions he has a right to use them, to do or leave undone, according to his 'free will'—although that very 'free will' is over-ruled by the free will of God alone, according to his own pleasure. However, with regard to God, and in all that bears on salvation or damnation, he has no 'free will,' but is a captive, prisoner, bondslave, either to the will of God, or to the will of Satan."

While in 1525 it appeared as if Luther had been trapped between the battlelines of politics and of the spirit, he actually drew a line of demarcation which enabled him to concentrate his labors on building a new order of things.

The old order had largely collapsed. In October of 1525 Luther had written to the successor of Frederick the Wise, John the Steadfast: "Everywhere the parishes are in a wretched state! No one gives, no one pays. The pennies for the souls and the sacrifices have decreased. Income has dropped or ceased altogether, so that consequently the common man respects neither the preacher nor the pastor. Unless Your Electoral Grace boldly establishes a new order and undertakes to support pastors and preachers decently, nothing will be left of the parishes, schools, or pupils. And, consequently, God's Word and the service to God will fall into ruin." In view of these facts Luther recommended to the Elector that a visitation be organized to investigate the existing conditions. Subsequent to such a visitation and with the help of the Reformers, a new form of church organization was to be developed, new institutions created to replace those presently in existence. All in all, this suggestion assumed the likely alliance between the new church—still to be structured—and the sovereign of the territorial state. With Elector John's approval, the electorate was now divided into visitation districts. Melanchthon prepared a set of instructions for the visitors which was published in 1528 and then put into practice. Developing concurrently with this church visitation was the endeavor toward a basic reform of the schools. This involved the withdrawal of the school from its ecclesiastical context and its re-establishment as the responsibility of the communal authorities. In the future it would be the community that would have to bear and meet the costs of education. This program had already been promulgated in Luther's treatise of 1524, *To the Councilmen of All Cities in Germany That They Establish and Maintain Christian Schools*. But now the investigation of the school system was incorporated into the visitation program and action was taken.

As usual, Luther did not limit himself to the organizational aspect, nor did he entangle himself in rigid legal arrangements. Here, too, he put primary emphasis upon the living proclamation of the Word. He drew his own conclusions from the shattering results of the visitation and created one of his famous pedagogical tools: *The Large Catechism* and *The Small Catechism* of 1529.

In these two books he explained with vivid pictorial clarity and pedagogical incisiveness for his own and innumerable future generations what is meant by God's Word and command, by faith and the church. Luther's *Small Catechism* is a book which in its original version and in many later variants helped to establish a framework for the life of the Evangelical, to define ethical concepts, and to set up an order establishing the individual, within the fleeting changes of his particular times and needs, to keep his bearings. And all this with great simplicity, readable for young and old alike, easy to understand and to commit to memory!

Satirical caricature of Dr. Eck, Dr. Lemp, Pope Leo, and others, a contemporary woodcut.

Philip Melanchthon

In many of Luther's remarks one frequently comes across the name "Philippus," for that was the name by which Luther called his friend Melanchthon. In 1518, at the age of only twenty-one, Melanchthon came to Wittenberg as a professor. Luther and the other Reformers were quite shocked by his youthful appearance. Then the young man stepped to the rostrum, and after his first lecture the unanimous verdict was expressed: This man is going to reform the university and will bring about changes in its academic format. This actually happened. During the years 1520-1521 he wrote the first book of Evangelical dogmatics, his Loci communes. Speaking of this book, Luther said that one ought to forget all his *own books. It is only important that the Bible and Melanchthon's Loci communes continue to exist, for then justice would be fully done to the new teaching. Melanchthon's university reforms and the establishment of the Evangelical school system gave to the German university and the higher schools a design which endured until the eighteenth century.*

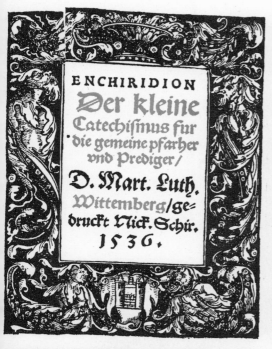

ENCHIRIDION
Der kleine
Catechismus fur
die gemeine pfarher
vnd Prediger/
D. Mart. Luth.
Wittemberg/ge=
druckt Nick. Schir.
1536,

Die Zehen
gebot/ wie sie ein
Hausvater sei=
nem gesinde ein
feltiglich für
halten
sol.

Ein Traw=
büchlin fur die
einfeltigen
Pfarherr.
Mart. Luth

1536

Das Tauff
buchlin ver
deudscht / Vnd
auffs new zu
gericht.
Mart. Luth

1536

ANNO AETATIS SVE 42

1532

John
Bugenhagen,
a 1532
painting by
Lucas Cranach
the Elder.

Doctor Pomeranus
(JOHN BUGENHAGEN)

While many of Luther's friends carried on their Reformation activities in other areas, John Bugenhagen often returned to this city. In 1523 he became the city pastor at Wittenberg, and later on he was also a professor at the university. He was the reformer whose activity covered the widest geographical area and whose organizational efforts had the most enduring significance. His relationship to Luther was unique, for he was Luther's father confessor. As a reformer in Brunswick, Hamburg, Lübeck, Denmark, and Pomerania, he also formulated the regulations of these territories for the church and the schools.

Luther and Huss administering the Lord's Supper in both kinds to the family of the Elector, a contemporary woodcut.

UBERIG SCHICZN

JR&GWADNHAS ZU FUES

UBERIG GHKZN

MFF DES REICHS OBRSST
VRTHAVBON
KAISERLICH MAJTT KONIGLICH M

DESS

HEILIGEN

REICHS

RAISIGEN

The Turkish Menace

During the first half of the sixteenth century no issue of universal political import revealed more sharply the backwardness of the governmental, financial, and military institutions of the empire than the conflict with the Turks. Seen against the background of the real facts, that is, the disunity among the states of Europe and the empty coffers of Emperor Ferdinand, the summons to the western world to unite in Christian oneness sounds almost like blasphemy. In spite of this, the attacking Turkish wave was twice broken at the gates of Vienna—in 1529 and 1532. For the next two hundred years, however, the Balkans remained in the hands of the Turks and the Magyars. Again and again the extent of the Turkish danger influenced the imperial diets in their handling of the issues of the Reformation. Under the pressures of the moment decisions were postponed. This situation lasted until Luther's death. Luther's position as far as the Turks were concerned was a purely spiritual one. Thus he wrote and prayed: "Christian must be the leader of this army. Truly, this struggle must be begun with repentance, and we must mend our ways, lest we fight in vain. How very much I would like to see Charles crush the Turks! With all my heart's desire I ask this of God. Yet whenever I lift my prayer, it sinks back again, for our sins are too numerous."

After the battle of Vienna-Neustadt in 1529 the victorious troops are presented to Charles V, a book illustration by Michael Ostendorfer.

191

Ulrich Zwingli,
by an unknown master.

Zwingli

The Reformation in the northern provinces and in the northeastern
areas of Germany was Lutheran in character, whereas in Switzerland
and southern Germany the Reformation was shaped by Ulrich Zwingli
and John Calvin. Zwingli was only a year younger than Luther. In
1506 he became pastor at Glarus, in 1516 secular priest at Einsiedeln,
and in 1519 he was called to the cathedral in Zurich. It was there
that he joined Luther's battle against the indulgences and interpreted
the Bible on the basis of the pure gospel. In 1523, with a mandate
from the Zurich city council, he inaugurated his program of reform
by abolishing the mass, dissolving the monasteries, and renouncing
episcopal authority. Soon, however, he followed another political and
theological path than Luther. After all, Zwingli's philosophy had its
source in his freedom-minded Swiss background.

The Cathedral
of Zurich,
detail from a
Panorama of
the City, by
Hans Leu.

Prince Philip of Hesse.

Justus Jonas.

Hoc est corpus meum—*This is my body*

Luther distinguished very sharply between that which is spiritual and that which is secular. According to Zwingli, state and church belong together. But more difficult than reaching agreement on these matters were the differences in their concept of the Lord's Supper. For Zwingli Christ was the lofty example and the Lord's Supper was a symbolical act. He could not agree with Luther's position. The increasingly adamant polemics on both sides threatened the unity of the Evangelical estates. Intent on the dissemination and safeguarding of the Reformation, Zwingli, in conjunction with the Prince of Hesse and the city of Strassburg, sought to bring about a coalition of Evangelical provinces against the emperor. The day could be foreseen when Charles V, following the final peace treaty of 1529 and relying on his newly acquired power status in Europe, would give serious thought to enforcing the Edict of Worms. It was vitally necessary for unity to be effected within the Evangelical camp. The religious colloquy, which the Prince of Hesse invited Luther, Zwingli, and their advisers to attend at Marburg from October 1 to 4, 1529, was to serve the cause of unity. At Marburg Luther adhered firmly and without compromise to the words which he had written in chalk on the conference table: Hoc est corpus meum—This is my body.

Panorama of
Marburg, by
Sebastian Münster.

194

MIHI PATRIA   COELVM·

Martin Bucer.

IOANNES · BRENTIUS · Theologus

Martin Bucer.

John Brenz.

The Minutes of the Colloquy

In the background of the Marburg Colloquy and its conclusion hovered the matter of an alliance of the Evangelical estates. Even though Luther had not yielded in the interpretation of the words of institution, he nevertheless recapitulated the results of the discussion in fifteen statements. Complete agreement had been possible on fourteen of these. As for the fifteenth point, all participants at the colloquy subscribed the following statement: ". . . Although at this time we have not reached agreement on whether the true body and blood of Christ are bodily present in the bread and wine, yet each party is to evidence Christian love to the other, as far as the conscience of each one will allow it. Both parties are diligently to entreat God the Almighty that by his spirit he may establish us in a right understanding." It was thus possible to continue unity talks. The situation, however, remained confused.

Signatures of the participants in the Marburg Colloquy of 1529 affixed to the minutes.

Charles V and Clement VII,
fresco by Giorgio Vasari in
the Palazzo Vecchio in
Florence.

Reconciliation Between the Emperor and the Pope. Emperor Charles Returns to Germany

Since 1526 Charles V had been involved in his second war against Francis I of France and his allies (the pope among them). The conquest and frightful sack of Rome by the German lansquenets in 1527 placed the emperor in a most favorable role in Italy. The victorious defense of Vienna against the Turks in 1529 also helped to strengthen Charles' position. The pope yielded completely. To cap his military successes, Charles had himself crowned by Clement VII in Bologna on February 24, 1530. The German electors were not present. Court members of the Spanish and Italian higher nobility performed the traditional duties of the court ceremonial and led the procession bearing the emperor's sword, the imperial orb, and the crown.

197

Augsburg

The decade from 1521 to 1530 was the politically formative period of the Reformation. The beginning was at the Diet of Worms, and Augsburg was the first concluding pinnacle. As interesting and as variable as the interim diets were—for example, the Diet of Nürnberg in 1523, at which the new pope, Adrian VI, submitted a confession of guilt in behalf of the Roman church, or the second Diet of Spires in 1529 at which Evangelicals were first called "Protestants"—we shall have to restrict ourselves to the Diet of Augsburg.

The emperor's intention of taking steps against the Reformation had been repeatedly thwarted by the political emergencies of the day. His foreign policy quite often provided the Evangelicals with an unexpected breathing spell. Such occasions were a confirmation of Luther's courageous faith, for he knew well and often testified that the mighty rulers of this world are merely figures whom God calls forth and directs on the stage of history. After the Reformation had passed the tenth milestone in the pages of history, the simple eradication of this "heresy" was no longer a possibility.

The diet scheduled to be held in Augsburg in the summer of 1530 was supposed to clarify the situation.

A special feature of this diet (which next to the Diet of Worms was the most momentous of Reformation history) was that Luther himself did not stand in the limelight, but had to entrust the representation and safeguarding of his cause into the hands of others.

This was the first major test. Since Luther did not personally participate in the decisive consultations at Augsburg, proof was now given to all the world that the Reformation was not Luther's private affair but concerned all of Christendom.

Since Luther had to remain at a distance from the diet (the imperial ban was still in effect and even the usually bold city of Nürnberg declined to accommodate him with lodgings), and since he could only follow the events from the distant Fortress Coburg, this diet can only indirectly be included in Luther's biography. He was kept informed of the situation as it developed—although much too meagerly and too slowly in his opinion. His advice was sought—he felt—too rarely and often too late. Divine providence had chosen other instruments beside him for this phase of the Reformation.

Luther himself did not view it differently. In spite of his impatience, as far as we can discern, he never for a moment separated himself from his colleagues who had to bear the brunt of battle at Augsburg, and above all not from his dearly beloved friend Melanchthon. Much nonsense has been written about Melanchthon's behavior at the Diet of Augsburg. The general opinion is that in contrast to the intrepid and forceful faith exhibited by Luther at Worms, Melanchthon demonstrated tactics of timidity and the dalliance of diplomacy. In response to this two things must be briefly said.

In the first place, Luther very obviously did not concur in this opinion. It is true that by innumerable letters he tried to infuse boldness of faith into the heart of the timid and hesitant friend at Augsburg. But it would be wrong to misinterpret his comfort as rebuke. On the contrary, it is proof of Luther's human greatness that he simply accepted Melanchthon's personality as it was. One should not misunderstand his famous opinion about the·Augsburg Confession, which Melanchthon had formulated after tedious political and theological negotiations: "I have read Philip's Apology. It appeals to me very much and there is nothing in it that I would change or improve. This would also not be the proper thing, for I cannot walk that gently and softly." This cannot be regarded as irony, but as the unenvious appreciation of a friend and his work. The final judgment of Luther about Augsburg is as positive as possible. Viewing the diet, he always saw as a reason for praise and gratitude that "the Word remained and we with the Word."

In the second place, Melanchthon from the very beginning regarded it as his duty to do all in his power not to make the threatening division of Christendom permanent and final. It was in this sense that he had accepted as *bona fide* the auspicious phrase in the imperial invitation which "desired to hear well-meaning opinions and thoughts of each person." The entire tenor of his theological statement offers proof that the Evangelicals had not established a new church. Originally he had planned only to speak about putting an end to the abuses in the church. The sharp emphasis placed by his opponents on the dogmatic schism, however, induced him to speak also about the articles of faith and doctrine which later on made the Augsburg Confession the classical document of Protestantism. For similar reasons the Elector of Saxony, John the Steadfast (Frederick the Wise had died in 1525), had wanted to see in the work of Melanchthon and his friends solely a Saxonian pronouncement. It had required a great amount of effort on the part of the other princes and cities to get permission to add their signatures, thus elevating the Confession when it was actually read at the diet to the status of a public confession. The contentious attitude of the other side also resulted in the Evangelicals' insistence that the credal declaration be accorded a public hearing. Their brave conduct won them a solemn reading of the document before emperor and empire on June 25, 1530. More as a result of the opposition of the opponents than because of the desire of the Evangelicals, the Augsburg Confession thus became the first public declaration of their faith.

The frequently misinterpreted attitude of Melanchthon shows that until the very last the Reformation sought to preserve the spiritual unity of the western world.

It must be stated very clearly that Luther had no objection to Melanchthon's attitude at Augsburg. Only in one point did he differ with his friend: He was convinced that unity could no longer be preserved, and his judgment was realistic. He regarded as mundane all the worries related to religious schism which a Humanistic spirit such as Melanchthon could not accept with indifference. If it was God's will to lead his Christendom into such hardships, then God's hand would also be able to preserve his church regardless of the future external forms.

The misinterpretation of Melanchthon is also unjust insofar as it unfairly belittles the acuteness and clarity of the credal assertions made in the Augsburg Confession. Article five, dealing with the "Office of the Ministry," is, properly understood, still a valid rejection of the hierarchical system of the Roman Catholic church. The last article, on "The Power of Bishops," though moderate in language, in its content, however, clearly points up the sharp distinction between spiritual and secular powers, which to this day has not lost any of its significance.

In the meantime Luther did not remain idle at Fortress Coburg. He was impatient, and this impatience vented itself in occasionally unjustified complaints about inadequate news reports from his friends. This is quite understandable. Likewise understandable is his constant endeavor to do all in his power to strengthen the faith of his brethren. To this endeavor we are indebted for some of the most magnificent expressions of his personal faith in the letters he wrote during this time.

In a sermon preached on October 2, 1530, two days before his departure from the Coburg, he once again expressed what it was that impelled his faith as he looked back upon the events of the Diet of Augsburg. The emperor and the Catholic estates of the realm had rejected the Confession, and the Apology which was to defend the Augsburg Confession against the reproaches of its antagonists had not even been officially received by the emperor. But the nascent Lutheran church was no longer in need of such defense. This inspired Luther to say in his sermon: "If they care to be gracious to us, let them be so in God's name. If not . . . what does it matter to us? Since the heavens are greater than the earth, it is hardly likely that the earth should govern the heavens. If they have in mind to do something, they will first have to ask our Lord God whether it pleases him. If it does not please him, then let them counsel and scheme all they want, for it is still written: 'He that sitteth in the heavens will laugh, the Lord will have them in derision (Ps. 2:4),' and in the end he will overthrow them. For he is the same God who has created the world out of the void, who gives life to the dead, and calls the things that are not, as though they were (Rom. 4:17)." Rulers and hierarchs may wield all kinds of temporal powers, but true faith must learn, as Luther once put it, "to stand on the void." But God who is able to call forth all his creation out of the void, is mightier than all temporal powers.

History has proven Luther's judgment of faith to be correct.

Copper engraving by Simon Grimm of the so-called *Fronhof*, the Bishop's Square, with the episcopal palace, containing the hall (to the left of the dormer of the central building) in which the Augsburg Confession received its public hearing.

Engraving showing the presentation of the Augsburg Confession in 1530. The Protestants had insisted that their Confession be presented not only in written form, but that it be read publicly—and in German—before the emperor and the empire. This took place on June 25, 1530, with the Saxon Chancellor Christian Beier serving as the reader. Although the emperor did not accept the Confession, he at least did not allow matters to conclude with the blunt alternative possibility: only a war can now lead to a decision. A council of the church was now to decide. This means that the cause of the gospel had remained firm. Everything remained in stalemate.

During Luther's stay at the Coburg Elector John Frederick presented him with a gold signet ring engraved with the Luther Rose. Luther had developed this emblem from his family's coat of arms and interpreted it as a symbol of his theology. Since the seal had been produced in Nürnberg, the town clerk inquired of Luther whether the finished product had turned out well. Thereupon Luther responded with the following letter:

The Luther Rose

"Since you desire to know whether my seal has turned out successfully, I would like to share with you in good fellowship the basic thoughts which I want to express in my seal insofar as it characterizes my theology. First, there was to be a black cross set on a heart which would have its natural color, in order to remind myself that it is faith in him who was crucified which saves us. For the righteous shall live by faith, namely, by faith in him who was crucified. The heart is placed on a white rose, to show that faith brings forth joy, comfort, and peace. This is why the rose must be white, not red, for white is the color of the blessed and of all the angels. This rose should be placed in a field tinted with the hues of heaven to signify that the joy and faith of the world to come have already begun to bloom here below. In this field there is also a gold ring, to show that the bliss of heaven endures for ever and knows no end, and that its joys and possessions are far above all earthly pleasures, even as gold is the loftiest and most precious of all metals."

Luther and
the Reformers,
painting by
Lucas Cranach
the Younger.
Erasmus is
included in
the group
composed of
Melanchthon,
Cruciger, Jonas,
Bugenhagen,
Spalatin, and
Forster.
Despite his
break with
Luther, the
respect and
admiration
inspired by
his scholarly
achievements
was so great
that he had to
be included.
This picture, a
detail from an
epitaph in the
Church of St.
Blasius at
Nordhausen,
was destroyed
during World
War II.

The Main Work Is Completed. The Entire Bible in German

For centuries the highlights of the early Reformation period—the publication of the Ninety-five Theses, the burning of the papal bull, the Diet of Worms, and the year on the Wartburg—have excited the imagination of people. These events were on the avenue of history. One of the momentous dates of intellectual history was the day in 1534 when Luther completed his translation of The Entire Bible. This accomplishment has given comfort and spiritual nourishment to the lives of many, and has helped to shape their lives. The most significant achievement of Luther's life had been completed.

Gottes wort
bleibt ewig.

Biblia/das ist/die
gantze Heilige Sch=
rifft Deudsch.
Mart. Luth.
Wittemberg.
Begnadet mit Kür=
furstlicher zu Sachsen
freiheit.
Gedruckt durch Hans Lufft.

M. D. XXXIIII.

Title page from
Luther's translation
of *The Entire Bible*
from the year 1534.

The *Smalcald Articles* best demonstrate how the political, ecclesiastical, and theological course of the Reformation moved steadily toward a separation from the old church and the formation of a new church. Now for the first time the newborn church of the Reformation stood face to face with the old church, and no longer halfway within it, as was the case at the time of the Augsburg Confession. Now for the first time it calmly surveyed the possibility or impossibility of a reunification and came to the conclusion that a historical rupture had taken place. Under the guidance of God the Reformation had become a *church*. It was no longer merely a reform movement within the Roman church, no longer only a theological "trend," no longer merely a German affair.

This situation was underscored by yet another fact. The *Smalcald Articles* were, in a sense, Luther's theological and ecclesiastical last will and testament. There is a curious parallel here to a previous occasion. Just as Luther could not be present personally at the Diet of Augsburg but had to stay at Fortress Coburg and from there pray for and counsel his struggling and confessing brethren, so now he was not able to present and expound in person the articles which he had written for the federal diet at Smalcald. When he arrived there in February of 1537, in the company of the Elector, he immediately became seriously ill. According to a report by John Mathesius he agreed to leave Smalcald: "Thereupon he commends himself (to God) in the prayer of the church and makes his brief and Christian confession, namely, that he would hold fast to the Lord Christ and his Word, that in his heart he acknowledges no other righteousness except the precious blood of Christ, which out of pure grace cleanses him and all believers of all sins. He then and there in the carriage makes his last will and testament." Those around him fully expected that he would die. The Elector, who had done everything in his power to save him, viewed his illness with such alarm that he arranged to have Luther's wife Katie notified so that she might see him before he died on the way. Luther himself was aware of the crisis. "All in all, I was already dead and commended you and the children to God," he wrote from Tambach on February 27. There, in the middle of the night, his illness suddenly took a turn for the better. That same night he wrote to Melanchthon reporting a miraculous improvement which he looked upon as an answer to the prayers of his friends.

"This example should teach us to pray and to dare to expect help from heaven," he wrote in the letter. His friends must have had similar thoughts when early on February 28 young Master Schlaginhauffen, who had accompanied Luther, returned to Smalcald with the jubilant shout: *"Lutherus vivit*—Luther lives!"

We return to the historical background. On November 7, 1536, Luther, together with Bugenhagen, had ridden to the electoral palace in Wittenberg in order to meet with Pietro Paolo Vergerio, the papal legate, who on the previous evening had entered the city with twenty-one horses and mules and had been welcomed with full honors by the Elector. According to an old account, Luther is supposed to have said during the ride, "Behold, there go the German Pope and Cardinal Pomeranus," and then to have added earnestly, "God's instruments." This meeting with a papal representative differed greatly from the one seventeen years earlier when at Augsburg he had prostrated himself at the feet of Cajetan. As the discussion at the palace proves, Luther had been clearly aware of his own course for a long time. In a subdued but forceful address he questioned the integrity of the papal plans for the council. Although Vergerio was an experienced, wise, and moderate representative of the pope, no agreement was reached. When the papal legate made his farewell, he was under the impression that he had been dealing with a "man possessed." And when he rode through the gates of Wittenberg, he had no idea that one day he himself would be an embittered foe of the papacy and would help to build the new church in southern Germany, in Switzerland, and the Tyrol.

It was obvious that the papacy was in no hurry about planning for a council. After some dillydallying it seemed toward the end of 1536 that a council might be held at Mantua in May of the following year. In order not to be caught unprepared, the Elector, at the beginning of December, 1536, charged Luther with the task of drawing up a number of articles which might serve as the basis for negotiations. In this beautiful letter the Elector requested Luther to write down his thoughts and belief in a godly writing upon which at the time of his departure from this world he would be able to stand and abide before God's almighty judgment. As early as December 18, when the treatise had grown to eighteen pages, Luther became ill and could continue his labors only by dictating his articles. But during the Christmas holidays it was possible to discuss the articles in a final session attended by Melanchthon, Bugenhagen, Jonas, Cruciger, Amsdorf, Spalatin, and Agricola. On January 3, 1537, the completed articles were submitted to Elector John Frederick the Magnanimous. Delighted with this document the Elector replied: "May almighty God through our Lord Christ grant us all his grace that with a constant and true faith we may remain firm in this and not be diverted from it by either human fear or opinion. But let us leave in God's hand all jeopardy and danger that may befall our country and nation, as well as our people because of it, for he has said that the hairs of our head are all numbered and that without his divine will we shall not lose any of them (Matt. 10:30). In all danger, he, to whose will we now desire to submit all this, will according to his divine will provide and arrange all things well for our brethren, for us and our children, our nation and our people. It is he who has chosen me to be a prince. If it be his will, he shall also preserve me in this state. If it be not his will, then all our worries about the danger will be to no avail. For as he deems it to be right, so will he do it." The Elector was also determined to commit his princely fellow believers to this clear and strong position at Smalcald where, at the beginning of February, the federal diet was to be convened.

The Elector's intention was never fulfilled. During Luther's illness the delegates to the diet heeded the advice of Melanchthon that they rest their case on the Augsburg Confession and its Apology. Thus the so-called *Smalcald Articles* were never actually discussed by those assembled at Smalcald, but were simply signed personally at the conclusion of the negotiations by the theologians who were present. But due to their importance they circulated very quickly throughout Germany and were added to the list of confessional statements which in 1580 were included in the *Book of Concord*.

The pivotal substance of these articles is to be found in the second part. After those matters have first been briefly enumerated on which no difference of opinion exists with Rome, the actual issues in dispute are briefly and precisely defined, beginning with the doctrine of justification, the mass with all its implications, monasticism, and above all, the papacy. The reader is struck by the calm, forceful clarity which throughout is intent only on stating a decision which has been made and which can no longer be reversed. The basic thrust is found in the resolute intention, based on the sense of pastoral responsibility, not to surrender the church to error. This is most evident in the question of ordination and the consecration of bishops. When the Evangelicals began to ordain pastors and call bishops, they did so not in a spirit of rebellion but out of a sense of pastoral concern and responsibility: Just because the church was in conflict with the opposing bishops did not mean that God's people would have to do without preachers.

Realizing the inadequacy of all efforts to restore the original ecclesiastical status, the papal church turned to the more burdensome and difficult task taken up in earnest eight years later by the Council of Trent: the Counter-Reformation. In the face of danger threatening them from the other side, the Evangelicals, for the first time, took the bold step of convening their own Protestant council to order and shape anew the faith and life of the church. The preceding year (1536) had seen the union with the Evangelicals from southern Germany in the Wittenberg Concord, which, after the failure of the Marburg Colloquy with Zwingli (1529), had now touched Luther most deeply. It seemed as if the time was ripe for a genuine and lasting union within the Evangelical camp. These glowing hopes were reflected in the articles which Luther composed, but they were never realized.

If we focus our attention on the one key idea which characterizes the position of the church in the *Smalcald Articles,* we can do no better than to point to the one thought which the Reformation itself never wearied of emphasizing over and over again: It never wanted arbitrarily to destroy an existing church and to replace it with a new one. The Reformation's goal was to restore the primitive Christian church, the church of the New Testament—return to the Scriptures, and to the ancient church and to the unequivocal acceptance of the great confessions of faith of the first three Christian centuries. This was a Reformation, not a rebellion.

Smalcald was known more for its political than for its church connotations. For a number of years the name was identified with the Alliance of Evangelical princes organized for the protection of the Evangelical provinces and cities. Although this alliance was not without blemish (Philip of Hesse, one of its leaders, is an example), it did represent one of the important political concepts of the Reformation century. The sphere of this alliance's influence extended to the point where later on even the Catholic dukes of Bavaria were accepted as members. But as the opposing confederation, the Catholic League of Nürnberg, also became stronger, things moved toward an inevitable climax and exploded in bloody warfare barely a century later.

During the fateful hours when the Turks threatened the empire, the Evangelicals remained loyal. Although Luther judged the danger from the Turks to be unusually grave, not a single word of his suggests that he ever considered taking advantage of this state of emergency. On the other hand, the policy of the emperor was motivated by the fact that for the sake of political unity he would also have to preserve the unity of the church.

It was not until a century later that church unity was sacrificed for the sake of political unity.

Luther, as a matter of principle, sought to keep the prime task of the Reformation—namely, the proclamation of the gospel in purity and clarity—free from all political objectives and thereby saved the Reformation. At Smalcald also he did not act as a spokesman for political ends, but endeavored solely to stand guard over the newly won pure proclamation of the Word. The effectiveness of his articles lies not in some inspired understanding of the momentary political situation, but in the basic clarity and perceptiveness with which attempts to exploit the Reformation politically were warded off.

The signature page of the *Smalcald Articles* and Melanchthon's handwritten explanatory comment. The signatures were not affixed to the original copy written by Luther, but to another one specially prepared.

The Last Years: 1535-1545

Even before the publication of *The Entire Bible in German,* Luther had set up a commission which met at regular intervals to review critically the translations that had been completed. This work continued for a decade, from January 24, 1535, to December 19, 1544. In some years the commission met four times each month. Thus the translation of the Bible commanded Luther's love, devotion, and diligence, as well as the linguistic skills and the knowledge of the foremost minds of an entire generation of scholars.

In addition to his biblical labors Luther continued his academic activity until shortly before his death. The last major lecture series on Genesis began June 3, 1535, and was not concluded until 1545. His academic obligations, however, were not limited to his lectures. He took very seriously his role as dean of the theological faculty and the matter of conferring doctoral degrees.

When speaking of Luther's labors we should not overlook the chores in his home, the former Black Monastery. When in 1524 it became increasingly difficult to raise the revenues for the monastery, Luther requested his ruler to use the monastery buildings for some other purpose and to assign him a room in another house. The Elector then gave the entire monastery to Luther without any further encumbrances. The document of conveyance, dated 1532, still exists. Little by little the austere old monastery was transformed into a dwelling place for the restless and extensive household managed by his wife. In addition to the parents, the children, the domestics, a manservant, an aunt of Katherine von Bora, tutors, adolescent nieces, and the sons of a sister, there were also refugees, nuns and monks, families of his friends and coworkers seeking asylum from the plague or epidemics. Not to be forgotten were the many guests, princes, officials, theologians, and scholars who wanted to see or speak with Luther in official matters or as they were traveling through Wittenberg. All were guests at Luther's table and some even stayed on for months as his house guests. Here there were wedding and doctoral dinners, or evenings devoted to family musicals. Out of all this coming, going, and sojourning, these domestic joys and worries, came the collection of Luther's remarks known as *Table Talk.*

The last years of Luther's life were filled with constant activity. Even during the last decade the annual journeys were a regular feature: the almost routine visits to Torgau, the circuit journeys of the church visitation, attendance at the assemblies of the Smalcald League, conferences on secular, ecclesiastical, and theological matters at one place or another in Electoral Saxony. To this must be added his voluminous correspondence. We know that on some days he wrote as many as ten letters by hand. The list of treatises that came from his mind and pen was lengthened considerably even during the last ten years. An enumeration lists about 165 works. There was no slackening in activity, only a shifting of accents. Luther's distaste for the manipulations of high politics, for the inflexibility of diplomats and jurists, increased. He was depressed to the point of being sated with life by the growing danger of war. As a matter of fact, five months after his death the Smalcald War broke out.

The final meeting of the Bible revision commission had taken place in Luther's presence in December, 1544. During the previous months in the course of one of his numerous journeys he had dedicated the first Evangelical church building, the Castle Church at Torgau. In March of 1545 the Protestants at the Diet of Worms declined to send a delegation to the council which convened at Trent December 13 and which inaugurated a new phase of the Counter-Reformation. In October Luther concluded his great lecture series on Genesis which he had begun in May of 1535.

The Conclusion of His Teaching Career

The conclusion of these lectures marked the end of his teaching career to which he had devoted himself almost without interruption since 1512. His last words were, "Here you now have the dear book of Genesis. May our Lord grant that after me it [the Exposition] will be accomplished more adequately. I am weak, and no longer able." A letter to Nicholas von Amsdorf mirrors his pessimistic and oft apocalyptic attitude toward the times and the future:

Wittenberg, June 3, 1545

"I am not interested in either diets or councils, for as far as they are concerned I no longer have any faith or hope or curiosity. *Vanitas vanitatum—* vanity of vanities. The Nürnbergers have succeeded in getting a nobleman into their hands and are hoping to exchange him for Baumgärtner [captured in a feud among the knights]. Unless God intervenes, this could obviously be the spark that might ignite a huge fire that would be a punishment of Germany. May God, before this time comes, save us and our loved ones from these afflictions. No justice—no government in the empire—an empire without sovereignty—the dregs and the end of the empire!"

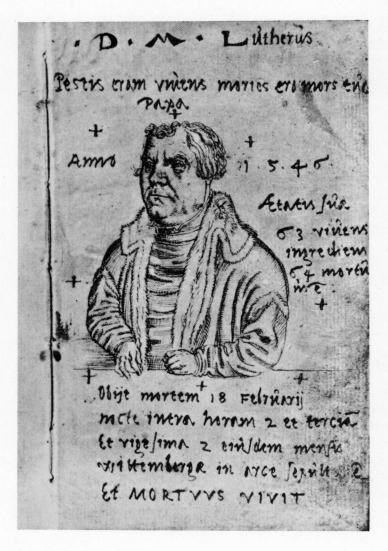

Et Mortuus vivit

The drawing on this page shows Luther on the lecture platform, produced during his last lectures in 1545 by Reifenstein, his amenuensis, on the inside cover of a book that belonged to Melanchthon. The written comments are by Melanchthon and deal with Luther's age, his death, and his burial. They conclude with a eulogy: ET MORTUUS VIVIT—AND THOUGH HE BE DEAD, HE LIVES.

Luther in the vineyard of the Lord, detail from a painting by
Lucas Cranach the Younger.

The Last Journey

Luther had an excellent reputation among his contemporaries as a mediator
and counselor. Despite his age and ill health he could not turn a deaf
ear to a request that he arbitrate a legal and family quarrel of long standing
involving his former sovereigns, the counts of Mansfeld. On January 23,
1546—a bleak time of the year—he departed from Wittenberg with his
three sons and his servant John, for Eisleben, where the negotiations were
to take place. The Saale River had become impassable because of ice and
floods. He was therefore detained in Halle for three days. When he con-

tinued his journey he was joined by Justus Jonas and at the boundary of the Mansfeld territory they were met by an honorary escort of 113 riders. Shortly before reaching Eisleben he was stricken with a spell of weakness. Yet on January 31 he was again able to occupy the pulpit at Eisleben. The negotiations had begun on January 29 but progress was slow. During this time he preached four times, administered communion, and ordained two clergymen. His skill as a conciliator was greatly taxed in bringing about a legal and honorable settlement between the two counts, but finally he was successful.

On the following day, February 17, the issue was settled, and an accord, reached as a result of Luther's effort, was also signed by him. That same evening his friends recognized signs of an impending physical collapse. During the night his illness became worse.

The castle at Mansfeld, detail from a copper engraving by Matthew Merian.

ANNO ÆTATIS. 50   1543

Martin Luther, a 1543
miniature from the
so-called Memory
Album of Lucas
Cranach the Elder.

Those around him recognized the danger of the situation and sent for the doctor who tried in vain to strengthen the waning life pulse. They could still hear him pray. His companion Justus Jonas has recorded what Luther said: "O my heavenly father, God and father of our Lord Jesus Christ, O God of all comfort, I thank you that you have revealed your dear son to me, in whom I have believed, whom I have preached and confessed, whom I have loved and praised, whom the dreadful pope and all the godless dishonor, pursue, and revile. My Lord Jesus Christ, I commend my soul to you. O heavenly father, I know that even though I am separated from this body and torn out of this life, I yet know as a certainty that I shall live with you eternally and that no one shall be able to pluck me out of your hands.' Several times he prayed the verse from the office of compline: "Into Thy hands I commend my spirit, O faithful God." His two most devoted disciples and colaborers called to him, "Reverend father, are you ready to die trusting firmly in your Lord Jesus Christ and in the doctrine which you have taught in his name?" He answered "Yes" with clear voice, and soon thereafter "died peacefully and gently in the Lord, as Simon sings."

The Last Picture

Immediately after Luther's death the counts of Mansfeld sent a messenger on horseback to Halle to fetch the painter Lucas Furtenagel. His sketch is the only authentic depiction that we have of the Reformer in death, since the death mask which had been prepared in Halle during the solemn procession on the way to Wittenberg, was altered during the Baroque period for reasons unknown to us today.

Luther in death, drawing by Lucas Furtenagel.

ORAVIT, DOCVIT, CHRISTVS, FIT VICTIMA, VICTOR.

Das newe Testament.
auffs new zugericht.

I.N.R.I.

Doct: Mart: Luth:
Witeberg.
Gedruckt durch Hans Lufft.
1 5 4 6.

VETVS ⎫
NOVVM ⎭ testamentum est ⎧ FONS ⎫
⎩ LVX ⎭

Title page
from the
last edition
of the New
Testament
reviewed
by Luther,
printed in
1546 by
Hans Lufft
at Wittenberg.

Luther's Legacy

The accounts of his life which were prepared immediately after his death reflect the awareness that a great life had now come to its end. Nevertheless, these accounts cannot do complete justice to the thoughts which his death engenders.

The Luther who died at Eisleben, almost twenty-five years after the Diet of Worms, was no longer the popular hero and the widely esteemed focal point of historic decisions. One could easily get the impression that much workaday drabness surrounded his person. He had aged, had gained weight, and had been plagued by many physical ailments. The world in which he had to live no longer looked rosy to him. For him, as for everyone, this world had more disappointments in store than hopes. The chapter of the Reformation which ends with his death seems so completely immersed in the colorless light of resignation, that the world of the church and the spirit in general, yes, to a certain extent, also the world of scholars, has turned away from the picture of the "old Luther" because it is not very appealing.

But that is certainly wrong. A rebuttal to such a viewpoint might best be expressed thus: The historic greatness of the "old Luther" lies in the fact that up to the last day of his life he *lived* unswervingly on the basis of the insight which he had recovered and taught: God justifies sinners. It is this sobermindedness which confers a greatness upon his later years.

The same inspired sobermindedness obtains in his plans for the new church order. These have nothing in common with the flaming emotionalism of the "enthusiasts." The very fact that since the extensive church visitation of 1529 he continually stressed the need for religious instruction, proves that he had no illusions about the people with whom he had to deal. He regarded them not as harbingers of the communion of saints, but as illiterates and dullards in need of instruction and preaching. More than once he stated that the orderly instruction of youth bears fruit and vexes the devil. He admonished parents, teachers, and magistrates faithfully to fulfill their obligations to the young generation. On the other hand, however, he realized just as clearly that the world would not be transformed in some magical way just because Christian sermons could be heard in it. He knew that the gospel would be in a continual state of war with Satan until the end of time.

220

He was certainly not a pedantic schoolmaster who wanted to regulate life down to the most minute details. He was willing to allow those things to exist and grow which do no harm to the gospel. In fact, we see in him a man who inspires us to remember God's forgiving mercy. In this world there can never be any order which fully and exclusively represents God's holy will. All that is reserved for the world to come and for the present we must be content to live in a world in which God's sun shines upon the just and the unjust. But every person who recognizes his own constant need of forgiveness will also know exactly where we owe one another forebearance and forgiveness.

Nor is it true that in his theology the "old Luther" was not the same as he was at the beginning of his career. His theological position remained unaltered. All his life he promulgated only *one* theology: the theology of the cross. This remained the central content of his testimony, and was expanded by his ever-increasing eschatological expectations. Afflictions continue to be among the most essential signs of the true Christian life, just as persecution and oppression remain the most basic marks of the true church. But these signs are simply proof that the Christian and the church are treading the same path which their master took before them and for them—the road of suffering. Above and behind all these earthly hardships the great and eternal goal of history rises in light, the day of God toward which all temporal events are on the move.

Nor is it true that in his later years Luther's theological creativity diminished in quantity or quality. It was during the last decade of his life that he gave his greatest and most comprehensive series of lectures, the exposition of the Book of Genesis. Here Luther vigorously propounds some of his most essential theological concepts. During his last years his theology and his Christian life were fused into a unity. The vigorous "Yes" with which Luther, even in the hour of death, subscribed to his entire theological labors, completely dominated his Christian life as well. He was *simul justus et peccator,* both just and a sinner at the same time. He lived by virtue of God's justification of the sinner. This is the very reason why the aging Luther was so untheatrical. It is true that he had very exact ideas about his place in history, and at times he expressed these with utmost candor. But to the end he assumed no pose.

And not least of all, it must be remembered that to the very last Luther remained undaunted. It would have been perfectly normal if, under the duress of bodily afflictions and the manifold threats to his life's work, he had fallen prey to a mood of fatal resignation. But on numerous occasions he expressed the conviction that in the last analysis the enemies of the gospel would be unable to accomplish anything—for "he who is with us is greater than he who is in the world." "Christ is mightier than Satan."

The famous note found after his death contains the last known statement from his own hand and is like a summation of his life's work (see below). At its conclusion he writes of man's inability to fathom fully the depth of God's word, and that we can do no more than bow before it in awe. "We are beggars! That is true." This declaration stands, to be sure, in direct contrast to the posture of self-assurance assumed by so-called modern man. More than two centuries of the most recent history of thought have endeavored to proclaim and give reality to the theme of man's self-glorification. Today no one any longer doubts that this attempted rebellion on the part of man has failed. The individual, who had made himself the measure of all things, has now become unsure of himself, As never heretofore, he has become homeless in the very same cosmos which he wanted to control by his own powers, without God or ties to a world beyond. In the face of man's "achievements," which in the end have turned out to be a deadly threat to him, this final statement by Luther sounds like both an admonition and a warning: "We are beggars! That is true." But ultimately the importance lies not in the fact that we are beggars, for rising majestically behind Luther's last word is the faith in the God who is the hope of the lowly, the consolation of the sinners, the life of the dying, and who will fill the empty hands of the beggars.

Luther's Last Statement

On the table of Luther's lodging in Eisleben, a note was found which he had written the day of his death. It is the last written statement that has come down to us from him. It reveals his profound admiration for Virgil and the writers of antiquity. "Nobody can understand Virgil in his *Bucolics* (Shepherd Poems), unless he has been a shepherd for five years. Nobody can understand Virgil in his *Georgics* (Songs of the Country), unless he has been a plowman for five years. Nobody can understand Cicero in his *Epistles*, unless he has lived for twenty-five years in a large commonwealth. Let no one think he has sufficiently grasped the Holy Scriptures unless he has governed the church for a hundred years with prophets like Elijah and Elisha, John the Baptist, Christ, and the apostles. Don't venture on this divine *Aeneid*, but rather bow low in reverence before its footprints! We are beggars! That is true."

Sources of Illustrations

The publishers and authors wish to express their gratitude and appreciation to the following for their counsel, the lending of resource materials, and permission for the reproduction of the illustrations presented in this book:

Professor Oskar Thulin (*Lutherhalle,Wittenberg*)
Dr. Otto Beuttenmüller (*Melanchthon Museum, Bretten*)
Dr. Wolf Stubbe (*Graphic Collection, Kunsthalle, Hamburg, Foto Kleinhempel*)
Professor René Kende (*Hilden*)
Städtische Sammlungen, Augsburg
University Library, Basel
Collection of Engravings, Staatliches Museum, Berlin-Dahlem (*Foto Steinkopf*)
Coin Collection, Staatliches Museum, Berlin
Museum of Fine Arts, Budapest
The Trustees of the Chatsworth Settlement, Chatsworth, England
Staatliche Kunsthalle, Karlsruhe
The Louvre, Paris
The Prado, Madrid
The City of Söderfors, Sweden
Graphic Collection, Staatsgalerie, Stuttgart (*Foto Weizsäcker*)
Landesbibliothek, Stuttgart (*Foto Staatsarchiv and Foto Kilian*)
The Wartburgstiftung
Kulturinstituten, Worms
Schweizer Landesmuseum, Zurich
The publishers of the periodical *Die Waage*

Museum Photographs
Foto Städtische Kunstsammlungen, Augsburg (*201*)
Öffentliche Kunstsammlungen, Basel (*77, 100*)
Coin Collection, Berlin (*121*)
Melanchthon Museum, Bretten (*Frontispiece, 87, 108, 140*)
Devonshire Collection, Chatsworth (*50*)
Staatliche Kunsthalle, Karlsruhe (*134*)
The Louvre, Paris (*62, 94*)
The Wartburgstiftung (*98, 99*)
Lutherhalle, Wittenberg (*128, 169, 181, 204, 214, 215, 218, 219*)

Kulturinstituten, Worms (*10, 148, 149, 155*)
Schweizer Landesmuseum, Zurich (*193*)

Picture Archives and Other Sources
Alinari, Florence (*52, 63, 116, 117, 197*)
Archiv für Kunst und Geschichte, Berlin (*71*)
A. Y. R. Mas, Barcelona (*67*)
Ballerin Pressfoto, Heidelberg (*132*)
Klaus G. Beyer, Weimar (*109, 110*)
Bildarchiv Handke, Bad Berneck (*152, 186, 195*)
Furche Archiv, Hamburg (*47, 70, 76, 141, 161, 162, 164, 175*)
Foto Marburg (*18, 64, 68, 194, 195*)
Historia Foto, Bad Sachsa (*9*)
Foto Hahnl, Salzburg (*115*)
Hoffmann und Campi Archiv, Hamburg (*96, 97, 100-105, 216*)
Internationale Bildagentur Oberengstringen, Zurich (*137*)
Professor René Kende, Hilden (*51, 75*)
Foto Kilian, Stuttgart (*107, 122, 153, 156, 159, 167, 179*)
Foto Kleinhempel, Hamburg (*12, 49, 52, 53, 55-59, 69, 79-81, 83, 85, 95, 106, 110, 120, 135, 136, 139, 152-154, 165, 188, 189*)
Mathias Film, Stuttgart (Oertel Film, *Der gehorsame Rebell, 157, 192*)
Pergamon Archiv, Munich (*11*)
Sammlung Reinking (*160, 163, 180, 187, 202*)
Walter Steinkopf, Berlin (*60, 61, 190, 192*)
Staatsarchiv, Stuttgart (*148, 151, 194, 217*)
Ullstein Bilderdienst, Berlin (*88*)
Foto Universitätsbibliothek, Basel (*73*)
Württembergische Landesbildstelle, Stuttgart (*182*)
Foto Weizsäcker, Stuttgart (*42, 43, 82, 111, 123, 126, 185*)
Foto Zierow, Heidelberg (*161, 206, 211*)